THE TEREZÍN ALBUM *of* MARIÁNKA ZADIKOW

THE TEREZÍN ALBUM *of* MARIÁNKA ZADIKOW

Introduction and Annotations by Debórah Dwork

The University of Chicago Press

Chicago and London

Mariánka Zadikow May was born in Germany and fled to her mother's native Czechoslovakia when she was a girl. She and her family were deported to Terezín in 1942. After the war she relocated to the United States, and she now lives in upstate New York. *Debórah Dwork* is the Rose Professor of Holocaust History and the Director of the Strassler Family Center for Holocaust and Genocide Studies at Clark University. She is the author or coauthor of many books, including *Children With A Star: Jewish Youth in Nazi Europe, Holocaust: A History,* and *Auschwitz: 1270 to the Present.*

The University of Chicago Press, Chicago 60637
The University of Chicago Press, Ltd., London
Introduction and annotations © 2008 by Debórah Dwork
© 2008 by The University of Chicago
All rights reserved. Published 2008
Printed in China

16 15 14 13 12 11 10 09 08   1 2 3 4 5

ISBN-13: 978-0-226-51186-3 (cloth)
ISBN-10: 0-226-51186-3 (cloth)

Library of Congress Cataloging-in-Publication Data
May, Marianne Zadikow, 1923–
The Terezín album of Mariánka Zadikow / Marianne Zadikow May ;
introduction and annotations by Debórah Dwork
　　p.　cm.
Includes bibliographical references.
ISBN-13: 978-0-226-51186-3 (cloth : alk. paper)
ISBN-10: 0-226-51186-3 (cloth : alk. paper)
1. May, Marianne Zadikow, 1923– .
2. Holocaust, Jewish (1939–1945) — Germany—Personal narratives.
3. Theresienstadt (Concentration camp) I. Dwork, Debórah. II. Title.
DS134.42.M39A3 2007
940.53'18092—dc22
[B]   2007024206

PHOTOGRAPHY: MICHAEL TROPEA

♾ The paper used in this publication meets the minimum requirements of the American National Standard for Information Sciences—Permanence of Paper for Printed Library Materials, ANSI Z39.48-1992.

Contents

Publisher's Note

The translations in this volume were prepared by Marianne Zadikow
May with the assistance of Tatyana Macaulay. They are not professional
translations but are true to Mrs. May's voice and to her memory of those
who inscribed her *Poesiealbum.* The *Poesiealbum* is not reproduced here in
its entirety; several postwar entires have been omitted. The transcriptions
of the handwritten texts reproduce the indiosyncrasies of their orthography,
punctuation, and capitalization.

The University of Chicago Press thanks Miriam Bratu Hansen for bringing
this work to the Press, Debórah Dwork for her scholarly contribution to the
project, and Marianne Zadikow May for her patience and generosity of spirit.

Introduction   <small>DEBÓRAH DWORK</small>

Luck and fortuitous circumstance saved Mariánka Zadikow's life. Music saved her soul. "I am," she said more than half a century after liberation from the transit camp the Germans called Theresienstadt, "a *Requiem* survivor. I'm not a Holocaust survivor; I am a *Requiem* survivor." If she had managed to weather the storm of the Nazi era by chance—including at one point, a mere clerical error—her participation in Verdi's *Requiem* under the direction of fellow inmate Rafael Schächter had kept her whole. "I survived with, because of, and after *The Requiem*. I, therefore, am a *Requiem* survivor."[1]

Born in Munich on 26 May 1923, Marianne (as she was called in Germany) enjoyed a rich and unusual childhood. "My home life was different from anybody else's," she recalled. Her father, the sculptor and portraitist Arnold Zadikow, commanded respect in the art world and renown among clients. Her mother, the artist Hilda Lohsing, did a lively business on commission in a range of media, from painted furniture to handmade lampshades to embroidered and batik piano covers. Marianne's earliest memories date from the family apartment in Munich, with living quarters for the three of them on one floor and her father's studio at the top of the building. "The entire ceiling of his studio was glass, and the north wall was glass."

Yet in many respects Marianne's family was very much like that of other children. Like other fathers, Arnold took his child to the park. Like other mothers, Hilda cooked festive dinners. Marianne was part of a family circle, and her parents took her to meet the relatives. Her mother came from Prague, and twice in the ten years the family lived in Munich, Marianne went to Prague "to visit my old grandmother and to meet some of my mother's cousins." Many summer vacations were spent in the Austrian Alps with her Prague grandmother, her maternal uncle Ernst Lohsing, a lawyer in Vienna, and her mother. She traveled to her father's family in Kolberg, too, to celebrate her grandfather's eightieth birthday "in 1928, when I was five years old. He still had an incredibly beautiful deep bass-baritone voice and sang a lovely, lovely German love song with an unbelievable amount of enthusiasm."

A cantor from Kovno, Lithuania, who had immigrated to Germany as a very young man, Arnold's father passed his passion for music to his son. After his father died, Arnold went to synagogue once a year, on Yom Kippur, to say Kaddish for him. For the Zadikow family in Munich, Judaism meant celebrating the holidays with friends, a full dinner, and singing. "My father had a guitar and a beautiful natural baritone voice." He sang Jewish songs, some of which his father had written, and "he would sing all kinds of other songs, including Italian love songs. I didn't know where one language started and another one ended. A Jewish holiday always ended with international music."

Marianne acquired another understanding of Judaism when Hitler came to power in January 1933. At that time, the German academic year began on May 1. Marianne had started school in 1930, a few weeks shy of her seventh birthday. She attended the Hohenzollernschule, where "there were hardly any Jewish children. I think in a class of forty-eight, I believe there were two Jewish girls." This made no difference until the new school year started in May 1933. "On the way to school, I was frequently—not just once or twice, but more than that, at least five times—beaten up by groups of three and five children, taller than I was. I had no fighting spirit. I cried and said, 'Please let me go. What did I do?' Well, they let me know what I did. They called me ugly names, like *Saujud*, dirty, dirty Jew."

These humiliating incidents led—oddly—to yet another, and very positive, understanding of what it meant to be a Jew. Religious education was part of the school curriculum: a priest taught Catholic students, a minister, Protestant students, and a rabbi, one Dr. Rosenfeld, the Jewish students. "This small giant, Dr. Rosenfeld, sat behind his desk and said, 'I am your uncle. We [Jews] are all related.'" This was a new and most comforting thought and, as Marianne learned, they had more in common than she had

imagined. Did the students have anything to tell, Dr. Rosenfeld asked at the start of each class. "To my greatest surprise, a lot of the other Jewish boys and girls in other classes had also been beaten up on the way to school." And they all had thought they "had to just shut up about it." Dr. Rosenfeld offered an alternative:

Dr. Rosenfeld said, "Here you don't shut up. You do not have to hold anything back, but you have to learn something." I remember myself saying, "I'm very sorry. I cried. I didn't know how to fight back."

"Good! Crying is not a shame, not at all. It's a normal reaction. What else can you do? But don't be angry. For they are so much younger than we are. They are thousands of years younger than we are. . . . So let's just think about this when we meet and talk about it, because it should be talked about. Good and bad things must be shared by a family."

Dr. Rosenfeld's "philosophy and teaching has accompanied me my entire life. When I was lucky enough, in a concentration camp during the Holocaust, to meet people I felt very close to, I thanked Dr. Rosenfeld, and I said, 'Yes. We are a family.'"

Membership in this family, a new sense of belonging, did not protect Marianne from the Nazi regime. The abuse she endured at the hands of gentile German children was but the first and by far not the worst of the ever more forceful attacks that would batter her, her family, and her community. "The thousand-year history of the German Jews has come to an end," the scholar, reform rabbi, and teacher Leo Baeck announced to a meeting of Jewish communal organizations shortly after Hitler had come to power.[2] He was correct. The thousand-year history of which he spoke had come to an end, and what is alive now is growth from a different branch of the tree of Jewish life in Europe.

But at the time, no one, not even Leo Baeck himself, realized how truly he spoke. Indeed, he dreamed of deliverance. "My idea is still this," he mused more than a year later, "I wake up one day and find on the billboards posters with the imprint: 'I have taken over executive power—General von. . . .'"[3]

European Jews had learned from their history that bad times come and go. Antisemitism was hardly new. Pogroms had raged through Jewish communities in the East just fifteen years earlier following the First World War, the Russian Revolution, and the reconfiguration of Central Europe. Antisemitic legislation had been a staple of civil life in many parts of Europe barely a century earlier. Thus, Jews—in this case, German Jews—had learned both to cope with antisemitism and to battle it as best they could. Their strategy in 1933 was shaped by historical experience: to hold on and hold out; to press for more and make do with less.

Passionately attached to their homeland and their nation, the 500,000 Jews of Germany in 1933 were baffled and bewildered by the ferocity of National Socialism. The great majority, like Arnold Zadikow, had been born and educated in Germany. They—again, like the Zadikow family—were not at all Orthodox in their religious observance and they lived in big cities. They saw themselves as part of the fabric of German life; they felt they belonged and they believed they belonged. Of course, how German Jews felt made no difference. Thousands upon thousands lost their jobs within weeks, and the daily life of virtually every Jew in Germany had altered within half a year.

This dissonance between the German Jews' sense of belonging and their rejection by German government and society gave rise to fear and despair. A record number of Jews committed suicide during Hitler's first year in power. Others, with more options, fled. They were for the most part politicians, professionals, intellectuals, and businessmen who had international contacts to help them leave.

Marianne, Hilda, and Arnold Zadikow were three of the some 37,000 Jews who found refuge elsewhere. Arnold was to have left first. "He had fought in World War I," Mariánka recalled nearly sixty years later, and he had sus-

tained grave wounds. When Nazi men began to parade about, well before 1933, Arnold had felt compelled "to stop whatever he could. He would stop Hitler-Jugend men in the street and tear off their swastikas and step on them, and say, 'Where were you, young man, when I had half my back shot out?'" When Hitler came to power, Arnold was a known opponent of the party. Plainclothes policemen watched the Zadikow house, and the family realized they had to leave. With his resources and reputation as a sculptor, Arnold Zadikow thought to go to Paris. As it transpired, his wife and daughter fled to Czechoslovakia first. The Prague relatives had become increasingly nervous about their Munich family's welfare since the shocking one-day boycott of Jewish-owned shops and businesses ordered by the Nazi regime on April 1. They prevailed upon Hilda to return to her native city and try to earn a living there. For ten-year-old Marianne, it was an abrupt end to the life she knew.

Hilda's former art teacher had left instructions in her will for her home to serve as a hostel for past pupils visiting Prague. Hilda secured a room there. For three years mother and daughter lived in a tiny, dark room, with a reapplication petition to the board of governors due every two months. Arnold, in the meantime, made it to Paris. Neither parent earned enough to support all three, nor was there money for visits. Hilda suffered from glaucoma and underwent a series of eye operations. Anxious and lonely, Mariánka (her new Czech name) found life rather grim.

A friend's generosity reunited the family in 1936. According to Mariánka, a well-to-do Parisian friend of her father's, Lucien Gerschel, bought him a ticket to Prague. The visit grew roots when Hilda, ever resourceful, introduced her husband to Egon Ritter, the manager of the famous Moser Glassworks in Karlsbad. She had done some work for Moser while still in Munich, and she imagined that the company could use Arnold's talents. She was right. "My father made a few drawings, right there, from the top of his head. Mr. Ritter was totally thrilled. My father was less thrilled. He liked Mr. Ritter, but he did not think an artist should stoop down to glass." An internationally renowned sculptor, recipient of prestigious prizes, Arnold Zadikow could not see himself as a glass decorator. His wife, by contrast, saw an opportunity to keep the family together. Arnold Zadikow took the job; he became Moser's artistic director.

"Life changed completely in 1936," Mariánka explained. "Now we were united. We also got an apartment." During the week Arnold stayed in Karlsbad, "and every weekend my father came." This meant much more than escape from the one dark room and meals cooked on an illicit single-ring hotplate. "I was already thirteen and I had a father again. And more music came into my life." For Mariánka, music signified love. Every weekend, her father "took out his guitar and played folk songs and Jewish songs and Hebrew songs and Italian songs and love songs. There was music again." For a time, music filled her life. "You can't live in Prague without music as part of your daily life." She took piano lessons, went to concerts, sang in a children's opera, and simply "stood still under a window [when] somewhere somebody was practicing piano, or violin, or singing."

The stability for which they had yearned and had sacrificed so much to achieve lasted less than three years. In Hitler's time, calm and tranquility, however carefully constructed, evaporated abruptly. For the Zadikows, as for many other Jews, the Germans' march into the German-inhabited perimeter of Czechoslovakia known as Sudetenland dealt a shattering blow. Britain, France, and Italy handed Sudetenland to Germany in the hope of "peace for our time," as British Prime Minister Neville Chamberlain put it after meeting with Hitler in Munich. With it, they also handed the Nazi regime power over the Jews in that area. Arnold Zadikow lived in Prague, but Karlsbad was in Sudetenland, and the Moser Glassworks was located in Karlsbad. He lost his job.

Sudetenland had become part of the Greater German Reich; Czechoslovakia's other lands, Bohemia and Moravia, as yet had not. But the Czechs, ready to wage war against Germany before Munich, now lost the courage to hold on to what was left. Resolutely anti-German, President Beneš resigned. So did the rest of the country. The leading liberal daily paper spoke for many on 4 October 1938. "If we cannot sing with the angels, we shall howl with the wolves." Force, not law, ruled the world; the Czechs would do well to find their place among the powerful. "Let us seek—we have no other choice—accommodation with Germany."[4] The new president, Emil Hácha, tried to do just that.

Hitler demanded no less. Prague must take orders from Berlin on matters of foreign policy, Czechoslovakia must reduce its army, limit freedom of the press, adjust its economy to suit German needs, and introduce anti-Jewish legislation.[5] Arnold Zadikow did not imagine that the Germans would march into the rest of Czechoslovakia, but "he wanted out as quickly as possible." Like hundreds of thousands of Jews across Europe, Arnold "wrote to everybody, even to Israel, which was Palestine yet—and he was not a Zionist. . . . 'Please help me,'" Mariánka recalled. Perhaps in response to these pleas, or possibly through connections among his artistic patrons, it seemed at one point that Arnold had secured an affidavit and a visa surely would follow. It didn't. The transaction called for a large sum of money, which the family did not have. That escape route vanished.

The family remained in Prague. Antisemitic agitation abounded. Hácha was summoned to Berlin in March 1939 to sign a German-drafted declaration stating that "the Czechoslovak President . . . confidently placed the fate of the Czech people and country in the hands of the Führer of the German Reich."[6] The German army marched in the next day, imposing a "protectorate" upon the remaining Czech lands of Bohemia and Moravia. The Nazis and their "Jewish Question" and their systems to "solve" that "problem" had caught up with the Zadikows.

"That was the beginning of the end," Mariánka recalled, with the benefit of hindsight. At the time, neither she—nor even the Germans—knew what the end might be. But conditions in March 1939 weighed heavily enough.

Uncertainty prevailed. The Zadikows had some money saved from her father's Moser salary, which "of course we didn't put into the bank. We put it under the mattress or into the shoes or under the coal bin. We knew, because of Austria, bank accounts may be closed." The question loomed: how to make a living? The Germans had closed the Jewish old-age home, and Mariánka's grandmother was thrown out. Her uncle Ernst had fled to Prague from Vienna months earlier. "My mother worked for the livelihood of herself, her husband, her mother, and her brother—five people—with maybe 60 percent vision if you take both eyes together." As resourceful as she was talented, Hilda taught several small groups of Jewish women every day "to become arts and crafts experts." These women aimed to emigrate. From Hilda they learned "to make handmade and hand-painted lampshades, to paint pictures, to draw from nature" to help them earn a living, should their unremitting efforts to get out of Czechoslovakia prove successful.

Hardship quickly overtook uncertainty. "Now comes nothing but restrictions," Mariánka explained. Higher education was out of the question and she became an apprentice milliner. Like many other Jews, including the women who took her mother's classes, Mariánka, too, took training courses. The Jewish Community Center offered this education, and Mariánka earned three certificates. "I am a fully qualified nurse for a newborn baby and to take care of the mother who was lying in." She also completed a course in early childhood development and another to be a laboratory technician. None of these helped her family to emigrate or enabled her to earn a living.

Mariánka, however, was adept and adroit. She, like others, "learned to do incredible things under incredible circumstances." A milliner named Friedl Dvorak taught her to make new hats and, as was more usual under the circumstances, refashion old ones. Dvorak, gentile and anti-Nazi, also engaged in her own form of regime sabotage. She obtained great quantities of "chicken, geese, butter, soap, green coffee (because you can smell roasted coffee miles away) on the black market." When the goods were on her premises, she told Mariánka and the other girls in her workshop that they

had to get rid of everything by morning. In Mariánka's memory, Dvorak took no money, or perhaps very little. This was her way of helping others. And Mariánka helped others in turn. She asked at the Jewish Community Center for the names of homebound elderly people whose children had managed to flee the country, and she took most of the food to them. Some items she sold on the black market, and some nourished her own family. She also "made money knitting things," and she did *Heimarbeit*, making artificial flowers at home for a German firm. "I never got any money for it, but I got my ration cards pierced. They didn't actually employ me. They gave me work to do at home. The Firma Wild, which needed these artificial flowers, gave out the work, and I had my card punched." This validation permitted her to present her ration card in the shops and buy the allowed goods, if they were available.

The family's efforts could not prevail against the ever-tightening stranglehold of the German regime. "The conditions between '39 and deportation to concentration camp were such that, in a way, you just couldn't [cope] anymore," Mariánka reflected.

You paid rent, but you're not supposed to have income. You can't get shoes, but your old shoes are finished, you're walking already on bare feet. You need medication, you could go to some kind of clinic where there was somebody who was allowed to give you a prescription. But how do you pay for it? Where is the money coming from?. . . The ration card you got at the magistrate building. And these cards also told you where to buy. . . . The intricacies of these things could make you nervous enough and upset enough to just say, it doesn't pay. I'll take my life.

But the Zadikow family did not succumb to despair. Like millions of other Jews, they carried on. When Jews in the Reich-Protectorate area were forced in September 1941 to sew a Jewish star on their clothes as an identifying mark, and shopping hours for them were set so late that nothing would be left in the stores, Hilda detached her star and went to the marketplace early in the morning. "My mother didn't have a good figure. She was wobbly. I helped her to pin a double pillowcase under her coat on her dress with three big safety pins. Into this pillowcase she would put all the vegetables she wanted to buy and in two shopping bags she would have a few potatoes here, and a few onions there. And come home." Mariánka flouted Nazi laws too. She continued to shuttle contraband food and fuel that she got from Friedl Dvorak. It was a dangerous activity. Her route from the milliner's workshop to her home took her through Prague's central Wenceslas Square, which was crawling with Germans. "Once I was stopped and forced to empty my bags, and I had coal with me. Out with the coal on the street. But I was lucky; they didn't do anything. After that I took side streets, but that wasn't safe either. In side streets, people do the same thing every day at the same time. And they see this girl with two full bags walking regularly down the street at the same time. Anything could have happened, but it didn't."

The Zadikows did not give up looking for an exit route. Arnold went to the Jewish Community Center every day in search of possibilities for entry visas, and off they rushed to apply. "We stand in line with every one of them. We can go to Lima, Peru. We can go to Uruguay. We can go to Palestine, of course. We were in all those lines." It came to naught. Just one option promised fair. In the months between the German invasion of Czechoslovakia and Mariánka's sixteenth birthday, she might have been able to leave Prague for England on a *Kindertransport*, a special rescue train organized to send endangered children west to safety. Countries that would not accept adult refugees were willing to offer asylum to children under the age of sixteen. Hilda registered Mariánka with the Quakers, one of the organizations centrally involved in this effort. But Mariánka did not want to go. She did not want to leave her family. Most especially, she did not want to be separated from her father again. "Now that I had my father with me, I should leave? I should go to England?" Mariánka remained, and she had more time with her father. "He would take me, in the very early morning hours, to the Moldau, and rent a boat, and we were boating on the Moldau with our breakfast. And this with a father I hadn't seen for three years."

6

* * *

Mariánka, Hilda, and Arnold Zadikow got their *Einberufung* (deportation call-up notice) in May 1942. "Three days later [15 May] we were supposed to be at a certain place at six o'clock in the morning, so no neighbor would see the people with the luggage and the knapsacks, fifty kilograms, twenty-five in each hand."

The Trade Fair Palace served as a central deportation point. Every transport was numbered, and each deportee wore a number on a string around the neck. "Our transport was Au-1. My number was Au-1 460. This is who I was. We were now nameless. We had lost our identity; we were only numbers."

At that point, the Germans did not yet employ cattle cars to deport Jews from Prague to Terezín. They left in ordinary passenger trains, and "we each had our own seat." If gentile neighbors and Jews who for the moment remained in Prague were deceived, so were those in transit. They, like all of Prague's Jews, did not want to leave their homes, their city, and the world that they knew. But they had no idea what awaited them just fifty kilometers away. "One of my very closest friends, Mirjam Kummermann, was in the same transport," Mariánka recalled. Mariánka was nearly nineteen at the time, and she "stood with Mirjam by the window, and looked out at the beautiful Bohemian landscape, seeing for the first time in years blossoming trees, mountains, fields, cattle. We were singing Czech folk songs together, as if [we] were going on a summer vacation." The train stopped at the small town of Bohušovice. Everyone was ordered off, and marched under Czech gendarme guard to the transit camp the Germans called Theresienstadt.

What was Theresienstadt? What purpose did it serve? In the spring of 1942 the Germans evidently made an important decision. They had murdered millions of Jews in the east. Western Europe's Jews must now be dealt with. But how? Perhaps someone suggested an annihilation facility in Belgium or France, but if so the idea got nowhere. Western Europe's Jews would be sent east.

This created the new logistical difficulty of moving many Jews over long distances. In the Soviet Union, *Einsatzgruppen*, the mobile arm of the Nazi murder machinery, killed Jews on the spot. There was no need to collect and transport people to annihilation centers. In Poland, ghettos served as storage pens. The distances to the camps were short and the authorities coordinated their activities. The situation was more complicated in the west, where there were no closed ghettos and Jews had long been integrated into society. Local sensibilities might be offended. Cattle cars in the central train station would not do. So the Germans sent Jews by third-class rail to an isolated transit camp within the country—and thence east. Thus, all except the by then rather routine initial deportation was screened from public view. No direct connection existed between the capital cities of western Europe and the new necropolises in the east.

The transit camps served another function as well. The often-competing agencies involved in the Final Solution shared a common policy of Judeocide, but each had its own agenda, priorities, and schedule. A round-up in Paris, for example, was not always coordinated properly with the maximum "legal" dispossession of Jewish property, the military's demand that week on the railways, or the current annihilation capacity in the death camps. Germans used the transit camps as holding pens for Jews until the gas chambers of Sobibor or Birkenau could accommodate them and empty railway cars could move them, thus maximizing the efficiency of the murder machinery.

Finally, the transit camps aided German subterfuge: these were permanent settlements, the Germans implied. In the case of Theresienstadt, the implicit was explicit. *The Führer Gives the Jews A Town*, proclaimed a Nazi propaganda film about that transit camp. The Germans' perversions notwithstanding, transit camps were not stable, merry communities; they were temporary, wretched stopovers on the way east. Indeed, many of the people photographed by the Germans had been deported and killed by the time the film was shown.

The Germans considered a number of options before they settled on Terezín. Prague's fifth district might have done nicely as a ghetto, but the Germans' desire for secrecy superseded the advantages of easy access. A number of other Bohemian and Moravian towns presented possibilities.[7] None so perfectly met the Germans' needs as the fortified garrison town of Terezín, where the Gestapo had set up its central prison in the local small fortress shortly after the Germans occupied the country. Built for military purposes by the Austrian Emperor Joseph II and named in honor of his mother, Maria Theresa, Theresienstadt was transformed into a transit camp over a century and a half later by Reinhard Heydrich, head of the Reich Security Main Office and Heinrich Himmler's right-hand man. By his order, the small walled city not far from Prague was evacuated of its 3,700 inhabitants and a "Jewish settlement" or "old people's ghetto" was officially established.[8]

A first transport of 342 young Jewish men, mostly construction workers, left Prague on 24 November 1941. Almost before they could begin their work, two transports of women, children, and elderly persons arrived. A second building detail was shipped in on 4 December.[9] Their job was to prepare for an influx of thousands. The newly established camp administration had far greater responsibilities. Like the Jewish Councils organized elsewhere, the Terezín *Judenrat* was composed of prominent Jewish men designated by the Germans to carry out their orders and to deal with the myriad problems of a community under duress. The council oversaw housing allocations, food distribution, hygiene services, medical care, and youth services; they established and maintained children's homes, cookhouses, a laundry facility, a library, a central bakery, thirty-six clinics, hundreds of sickrooms, and thousands of sickbeds. Created to "govern" the Jews, the German-imposed *Judenrat* had many responsibilities and great authority within the community but no power outside it and no leverage at all with the Nazis.[10]

Arriving in May 1942, the Zadikow family faced a streamlined reception system. The Germans shoved the deportees into *die Schleuse* (the "sluice"), the absorption depot located in the dank, subterranean dungeons of the ghetto walls. There they sat for a day or two, anxiously awaiting the Germans' next move. "We were still together the first night. The next morning we were roped up, all women and children on one side, and men on the other." Thus from one moment to the next families were torn apart. For weeks afterwards, family members did not know what had happened to one another.

Hilda and Mariánka were billeted in the Dresden barracks with thousands of other women. Each toilet was shared by "three or four hundred: you stood in line whether you had to go or not." They were detailed to a *Hundertschaft,* a work unit consisting of one hundred hours of unskilled labor. "You had to give one hundred hours or more to a very dirty and very disagreeable job, mostly cleaning something uncleanable with nothing but buckets, cold water, brushes, rags, and absolutely no soap or detergents or anything like that." Hilda was utterly unable to do such work. "I did two *Hundertschaften,* because I said to them, 'My mother had nine eye operations. . . . She has a very bad scoliosis. You're not going to gain anything by getting her. Please give it to me.' I did it. It was all right."

Like all the other inmates, Mariánka did not know how long even this filthy, backbreaking work would last. The inhabitants now understood that Terezín was a transit camp. In Terezín, the Germans' story of a permanent settlement had exploded in January 1942 with the first deportations from the camp to an "unknown destination" that month. These were followed by two more in March and seven in April, each train filled with one thousand people.[11]

The Germans who organized the deportations knew that Terezín was a transit camp. The Jews in Terezín knew it, too. But millions of other people did not. They believed, or chose to believe, the Nazi hierarchy's description of the site as an old people's ghetto. It was, the Germans claimed, a place where they, in their compassion, sent Jews unfit for the "hard labor" all the Jews "resettled" in Poland were to do. Thus Terezín helped to perpetuate the myth disseminated by Hitler's regime that the long trains of deported Jews were chugging along to agricultural settlements in the east, not to death camps. To avoid embarrassing questions, highly decorated or severely disabled war veterans also were eligible for Theresienstadt, as were a certain number of very well known Jews.[12]

Terezín, however, was hardly a settlement or a ghetto. As the statistics clearly show, it was simply another transit center. Of the 141,162 Jews shipped in, 88,202 subsequently were deported east; 276 were handed over to the Gestapo and then disappeared; 33,456 died; 1,623 were released to neutral countries (1,200 to Switzerland and 423 to Sweden) in 1945; 31 were let go; 764 escaped; and 16,832 remained, including 22 unregistered children born there.[13]

Oddly enough, the purely theoretical role of Terezín as a stable community affected inmates too. Despite constant threat of deportation, lack of food and hygiene, and omnipresent disease, the Jews created an intellectual and cultural life for adults and children. Initially the Germans forbade all such efforts, and numerous restrictions undermined the inmates' attempts. Deportees, as we have seen, were permitted fifty kilos of luggage, but only "essentials" were allowed, and neither musical instruments nor scores fit that category. Nevertheless, inmates organized cultural activities from the start. The first construction details included a number of musicians, poets, and actors; the cabaret artist Karel Švenk and the choir conductor Rafael Schächter among them.[14] Švenk's former career at the Club of Wasted Talent in Prague stood him in good stead in Terezín, where he established a cabaret and used his biting irony to mock camp life. Schächter organized singing evenings for the men in the *Aufbaukommandos* (construction details); later he would exert a profound influence on life in the camp in general, and on Mariánka Zadikow in particular.

Švenk and Schächter were followed by many illustrious artists and performers. Some, like Karel Froelich and Kurt Meier, smuggled in their instruments; others, like the actress Vava Šanová, had committed dramatic texts to memory. Each transport brought new talent. The inmates worked all day and—exhausted, hungry, the men separated from the women—some rehearsed in the evenings to perfect a performance for their fellow prisoners to enjoy. Scouts stood by to warn of approaching SS, and audiences were reminded not to applaud.

This pursuit of creative or intellectual endeavors took many forms. As the Germans strictly prohibited education, pedagogy went underground. The first so-called Elder of the Jews (appointed by the Germans), Jakob Edelstein, and indeed the entire Jewish Council, took child welfare seriously. Children accounted for about 10 percent of the population of Theresienstadt; the Germans (happily) took little notice of them, leaving their governance to Edelstein and his Council. They established a *Jugendfuersorge* (Youth Welfare Department) to safeguard the children's health and to continue their education despite the Germans' draconian prohibitions. To that end, the Jewish administrators supported a policy of instituting separate children's homes. Beginning in early 1942, children under the age of four lived with their mothers; after that age the majority were placed in a children's home, a *Kinderheim*. At that time many of the Jewish leaders were Zionists, and they had the idea that this collective life would help to instill the values of Zionism while protecting the children from the worst of the brutality of life at Terezín. In more prosaic ways, too, the Youth Welfare Department sought to improve conditions for children in the transit center. Their living quarters were less crowded than those of the adults. Late in the summer of 1942, the department prevailed upon the Germans to allow the children to use the courtyards and gardens (adults did not have that privilege for another two years); they even were permitted to play on the fortifications of the city. Within a few months the Council opened a children's kitchen that provided more and better-quality food, and early in 1943 it established a children's hospital.[15]

The most outstanding work of the department, however, was its support of clandestine classes. Secret study circles were established, and many of the *Betreueren* and *Betreuerinnen* (male and female child-care workers) in the homes were devoted to the cause of education. For them, as for the children, it was an act of faith in the future. Half a century later, Helga Kinsky-Pollack still had great admiration for the *Betreuerinnen* and the life they fostered in her room in the Czech home for girls aged ten to sixteen. Deported to Terezín in January 1943, Helga was among those who remained in the transit center; two thousand people from the same transport were sent on to the east immediately.[16] She was assigned to room 28 of L410 (house number ten on the fourth lengthwise street), the Czech children's home for girls.

We were a quite well-organized room, and maybe also a well-known room, the room 28 in this home. It was a very active room. We had a choir because our chief Betreuerin *[Ella Pollack, whom the girls called "Tella"] was a piano teacher and a concert pianist. She gave us tuition in choir, usually in* Evrit *[Hebrew] or in Czech. We were playing theater and celebrating Jewish holidays. Those were the biggest festivities to which we children looked forward. Our* Betreuerin *even managed to get food for us, special food which we never had otherwise, sandwiches and puddings, things like that. How she managed it, I don't know.*[17]

There were a number of possible reasons for the success of her group, but whatever the cause, this room of approximately thirty girls (the population fluctuated with the transports) and three *Betreuerinnen* was "a very close community."[18]

While the Germans never lifted their ban on formal education, their policy on cultural and scholarly activities shifted over time. The Jewish leadership, recognizing the importance of these activities to the camp inmates and worried about the risks entailed, quickly established a neutral-sounding department, the *Freizeitgestaltung* (leisure time activities administration). Housed in the buildings administration and headed by educator Fredy Hirsch and

Rabbi Erich Weiner, the *Freizeitgestaltung* got official sanction from the SS command in 1942.[19]

The Germans did not permit these activities in order to enrich the inmates' lives. Rather, this display of culture suited their propaganda program: toshowcase Terezín as a functioning, unexceptional city with a stable population and a normal civic life. Eventually they went to great lengths to perpetuate this myth. Starting in the summer of 1943, a coffeehouse, bank, post office, and even a petty crimes court were opened. Stores sold goods stolen from the newly arriving inmates; sometimes people repurchased their own possessions. Art and music in particular flourished. The camp boasted five cabaret groups, several small orchestras, a "municipal" orchestra of thirty-five musicians, and a jazz band. Lectures, poetry recitations, literature readings, and art exhibitions were warmly supported by the inmates. Just one of the many participants in the cultural life of the camp was the great scholar Leo Baeck, who had so accurately predicted the end of Jewish life in Germany in 1933 and so ardently dreamed of Hitler's demise. Baeck's family had fled to England, but he stayed in Berlin, believing that it was his responsibility to remain with his community. Deported to Terezín in 1943, the eminent and elderly rabbi worked indefatigably for the welfare of the camp inmates, including their intellectual welfare. And people flocked to hear him: his philosophy lectures attracted over seven hundred at a time.

The backbone of transit camp life, however, was work, not culture; deportation, not opera. Hilda and Arnold were fortunate: both worked as artists. Arnold was assigned to the technical department, located in Magdeburg barracks. One of his tasks was to create a model of Terezín that, as Mariánka has noted, still exists today in the camp memorial museum. The renown with which he came to Terezín and the useful skills he brought to the community not only protected him from deportation but also privileged his living conditions in the camp. "He got a very, very small room where some nice young men made a very simple, very primitive bed-like couch for him . . . with a straw-filled pallet. . . . The only disagreeable thing was that he was given a bucket and any human excrement had to be carried to the only toilet in this particular floor in the Hanover barracks. At least he was alone at night, not with hundreds of other people. And he could create what he wanted to create."[20] Hilda worked in the *Lautschwerkstette*, what the camp administration called a German enterprise. Under direct Nazi control, this workshop located just above the library produced items for "the German hausfrau, very quickly, very efficiently, in an enormous number," as Mariánka put it. "My mother worked there for quite a while, until the entire business collapsed. [She] designed covers for glove boxes, for telephone book covers, for bookmarks." Individual Nazis demanded things too. "Very often she would be called in the middle of the night. Her *Zimmeraelteste* [room boss] would come and say, 'You have to go to your studio. They want a painting done through the night. It has to be ready in the morning.' My mother made coats of arms for Nazis who explained that they came from some kind of noble family and their family coat of arms looks like this or that. Of course it was all imagination. . . . [But] she was not allowed to leave that desk until it was done. So my mother continued to work as an artist there under very, very extreme conditions."[21]

Protected by her parents, Mariánka worked at first with her mother, but that did not last long. At one point she was employed in the ghetto mental hospital, and in the summer of 1943 she was one of the people assigned to assemble and fill starting gear for motor vehicles "to prevent the machines from freezing. . . . It was on a conveyor belt inside a tent. That was for two or three months under horrible conditions. The noonday sun broiled down on us, and we had no time to go to the bathroom, or drink a cup of water, or anything. This was slave labor."[22] For the most part, however, Mariánka worked in the *Galanteriewarenerzeugung*, a workshop producing notions located outside the camp. Built by the Jewish Council, it was one of the enterprises they hoped would prove the economic usefulness of the inmates as a labor force for the Germans. "We made tobacco pouches for the German soldiers, and many, many other things."

However hard the inmates worked, however economically useful they proved themselves to be, was of no consequence to the Germans, who were not interested in keeping Jews alive—not even as a slave labor force. Conditions in Terezín conduced to death. With so many people crowded into such a small area and, despite the Jewish administration's heroic efforts, rampant hunger and a substandard hygienic infrastructure, contagious diseases abounded. Mariánka fell desperately ill in February 1943. She landed in the main hospital in Hohenelbe barracks. Suffering from pneumonia and pleurisy, she floated in and out of consciousness. But Mariánka was lucky. Medicine smuggled into the camp by a Czech country policeman, Karel Salaba, saved her life. Salaba hid Cibazol, an early sulfa drug manufactured by Ciba, and other medical supplies in straw mattresses to be brought into the camp. The medications were passed to an inmate named Annie Loebl, who gave Cibazol to Hilda for Mariánka.[23] Luck and fortuitous circumstance: Annie Loebl knew Hilda and Mariánka very well. Arnold Zadikow was not so lucky. He suffered a ruptured appendix, and was taken to the hospital too late for an operation. "I lay dying in one hospital and he lay dying in another hospital, and my mother after work went from here to here to here. The dying daughter here, the dying husband there. And on the third day, [8 March 1943] he died. He would never have died under normal circumstances."

*   *   *

The backbone of camp life may have been work but, for Mariánka and many others, music expressed its soul. Singing together with others pulled her through the misery of labor and the myriad harsh details of daily existence. It did not save her, but it kept her whole. Fortunately for Mariánka, shortly after she arrived in Terezín she met the alto Hedda Grabová. The energetic and talented Grabová had been deported in December 1941 and set immediately to organizing the women in her barracks to put on musical evenings. By all accounts a dedicated and committed musician, Grabová sought others who shared her passion. She approached Mariánka one summer evening in 1942 when Mariánka, feeling restless, was exploring the reaches of their barracks.[24]

I realized that there was a flight of stairs going up, and then from there, there was a narrow pathway to more steps. I tried to explore this because I didn't know what to do with my time. I didn't want to go to sleep. I came onto a huge attic. It wasn't divided into rooms. You could see the structure of the roof, and people in all kinds of corners who may be living there or sleeping there. But at that time there were spaces for groups of people.

This attic was humming with intellectual activities. Somebody had a speech about Einstein's theory of relativity. Somebody else about the mythology of Greece. Somebody else about the middle ages in Norway. Somebody else about pre-Communist Russia. Somebody else teaching a language, standing up with nobody having a piece of paper in their hand, just giving the words and repeating and repeating. "Repeat after me. I'll say this. Do you remember what we did last time?" Somebody reciting poetry. Languages I didn't know existed. I think I heard Greek for the first time. I know there was Russian, German, Czech, Evrit. Evrit spoken and taught, the new language of Israel, which didn't exist yet.

In one corner, an old woman (she was sixty) with white hair, who sang some old German songs and also taught a group of women. She taught harmony of music that is played in every synagogue every Friday night. She taught a group of women first the melody and then the harmony to it. And then the harmony alone and then the melody alone, and now together. Conducted the whole thing. I'm standing there, listening, fascinated.

I'm totally gone. I said, "This is going on here?" And if I hadn't come up here, I wouldn't even know about it. At which point, a heavy-set woman . . . looks at me and my enthusiasm. I haven't said anything yet. She doesn't know me from Adam. She gives me a little push and she says, "Do you speak Czech?" I said yes. "Deutsch kannst du auch? [German, too?]" "Yes."

She gives me a tiny piece of paper, rolled up, sticks it in my hand and says, "Don't show to anybody. Come there after working hours on your next day off." I said, "Why?" She said, "Do you like to sing?" "Yes." "Come."

Hedda Grabová served as "one of Rafael Schächter's talent scouts." At that point in the history of Terezín, Grabová looked for those "daring enough to do this" as well as potential ability. "We were not supposed to meet anywhere after work," Mariánka explained. "We were supposed to be in our barracks or in the street, or visiting our loved ones or fathers or brothers. But we were not supposed to meet anywhere in groups." And chorus singing, musical performance rehearsal, was "a group meeting."

Mariánka eagerly joined the others who gathered in the cellar of L410. "This was the very first time I met Rafi." Her esteem for Rafael Schächter still shone bright sixty years later. "A then maybe thirty-year-old smaller man with pitch black hair. With an enormous personality. A kind of ability to guide, to lead, to enlarge the enthusiasm that others already had." By the time Mariánka met Schächter, his productions had grown from informal singing to choral performances. Schächter now aimed to mount operas. He chose *The Bartered Bride* by the Czech composer Bedřich Smetana. Mariánka sang in the chorus. A comic opera which draws upon Czech folk songs and traditions, *The Bartered Bride* won the hearts of its audience in Terezín. "I sang *The Bartered Bride* twenty-eight times and was once an onlooker," Mariánka recalled. "I witnessed an unbelievable performance where there were actually people hanging from the rafters, standing, squeezing tightly to each other in the hallways of a former school. I was there. It's all true. Wherever you read it or whoever told it, it's all true. There was not a dry eye. People who spoke Czech and knew it was our national opera and people who had never heard it before, or had heard it only on the best stages of the world, everybody was equally impressed by it." Powerful as the opera was for the camp audience, prodigious as the demand was for it (one writer suggests thirty-five performances), for Mariánka participation in Schächter's productions "belongs to the most life-

giving, most reassuring, most positive experiences in my life. It became a quiet but very constantly existing addiction."

The Bartered Bride premiered in November 1942. "One operatic or concert performance followed another one," Mariánka explained; as they rehearsed one piece, "we were already informed what the next one would be. Many followed, including Smetana's *The Kiss* and Mozart's *The Marriage of Figaro* and *The Magic Flute*. Now part of Schächter's chorus, Mariánka sang in all of his productions. "It became for me the reason to get up in the morning. No matter how bad the job, and how inadequate the food, or the health conditions, if somebody got sick—I mean, all of these things happened. I have a list of things that I survived: this, this, this, this. The important thing was: but tomorrow is rehearsal. There is a reason to get up. It's like the religious Catholic or Protestant or Jew who says, 'tomorrow I go to church or tomorrow I go to temple.' [For me] there is Rafi, the guiding light. We're going to sing."

Cultural and intellectual endeavors cheered many Terezín inmates. And at the same time, they suffered from the harsh conditions of daily life. The Jews of Theresienstadt experienced both facets of their quotidian existence simultaneously. "Today, the milk froze in the pot," Gonda Redlich, head of the Youth Welfare Department, worried in his diary on 25 November 1942. "The cold is very dangerous. The children don't undress, and so there are a lot of lice in their quarters." Without pause or segue, he continued, "Today there was the premier performance of *The Bartered Bride*. It was the finest one I had ever seen in the ghetto." Redlich, too, participated in artistic endeavors. He supported these efforts to enrich the children's lives; as we have seen from Helga Kinsky-Pollack, this policy proved successful. And he had written a play for which the enormously talented musician Gideon Klein had composed the music. In his diary entry of 30 November, Redlich again moved seamlessly from the miserable difficulties of camp conditions to the artistic world. "An interesting and burning problem. Where to put people who will be coming? In the attics? But what will happen in the winter, in the severe cold? . . . I liked the rehearsal of my play."[25]

How to explain the role of music and other cultural and intellectual pursuits for the inmates of Terezín? It was not a question of transporting them "back or forward," but rather, Mariánka reflected, "into a realm of serenity or joy." If the performance was successful, "the room filled with poor, sick, old, starving, lonely people, these people had for an hour or an hour and a half with intermission, moments, glimpses of the past when they had been happy and when they had heard that same music. It didn't matter any more that their clothes were in rags and that their chair was a bad folding chair or a bench without a backrest. It meant that here was the music again."

Some felt that these performances—and the time and effort invested in them—constituted a popular forgetting; too audacious, they said; too unmindful of the inmates' plight. Such arguments were not unique to Terezín. "Theatrical Performances Should Not Be Held in Cemeteries," one Vilna ghetto leaflet proclaimed, for instance. Each time the matter arose, however, those who fretted ultimately recognized the value of yearning for a cultural life. As one initially harsh critic in Vilna put it: "And yet life is stronger than anything else."[26]

Still, when Rafael Schächter made plans, early in 1943, to mount Verdi's *Requiem*, a small storm broke. The well-respected musicologist Dr. Kurt Singer referred to this controversy in a review of the performance that was printed and circulated in the camp in October 1943. With such a rich religious literature upon which to draw (Handel's three Jewish oratorios were in the Terezín library) this piece should never have been performed, he wrote. Brahms's *Requiem* would have been the "right work . . . the fitting memorial piece for this place." Instead of the Old Testament text "How goodly are your tents, O Jacob; your dwelling places, Israel," [we heard] "Domine Jesu Christe eleison Agnus dei." And he wondered, "Didn't any of the responsible people feel this way?"[27]

Whatever they may have felt, argued, or discussed, Schächter began to work on this Roman Catholic mass for the dead—to be performed by Jewish slaves in a Nazi German transit camp. Only the four soloists had a score; none of the 150 choristers held as much as a slip of paper. They rehearsed in small groups, Mariánka's led by the bass-baritone Karel Berman. Karel, whom Mariánka came to call a "soul brother," was "a wonderful choirmaster." But Schächter inspired and led. "This is our rehearsal ground," Mariánka remembers Schächter exhorting the chorus. "After the war, we will meet once a year in Prague, in Smetana Hall. We will sing *The Requiem* there every year in memory of this year."

His dream was not to be realized. The premiere featured star soloists: Karel Berman (bass-baritone), David Grünfeld (tenor), Hilde Aronson-Lindt (mezzo-soprano), Marion Podolier (soprano), and a chorus of 150 men and women. Gideon Klein and Tella Pollack (Helga Kinsky-Pollack's *Betreuerin*) took turns accompanying on the piano. There was no orchestra. With the production successfully launched, everyone expected it to continue. But, as we have seen, nothing was secure in Terezín. Mass deportations in September 1943 brought a six-month period of relative calm to a crushing end. No transports had been ordered from March through August. Then, in one day, 6 September, the camp was devastated by the loss of 5,007 people, more than 10 percent of the total population. "A transport of five thousand people. They sent five thousand in one day," Gonda Redlich lamented in his diary. Families were targeted, and thus no age group was spared: 285 children under the age of fourteen; 3,925 persons aged fifteen to sixty; 797 over age sixty-one.[28]

Nearly all of Schächter's chorus was shipped to Auschwitz. Everyone suffered, everyone grieved; Schächter too, of course. But he chose to carry on. "Some said Rafi was going after *The Requiem* like a madman," Mariánka observed. "He was not a madman, but a dedicated man who had a mission. He would not be diverted from that mission by anyone or anything. When most of the choristers were gone, he said, 'Okay, we won't have what

we had before, but we will continue *The Requiem*. We must. We must."
Schächter trained the new group and again they mounted a performance.
And again the chorus was demolished with a transport to the east. And
again Schächter assembled a new chorus. "Three times during *The Requiem* [preparation], nearly all the choristers were sent away in a transport.
We had been trained for three-quarters of a year before we sang the first
time. And Rafael Schächter took it upon himself to train other groups."

The history of the choristers and the history of the German annihilation
machinery intersect at many points. As we have seen, Terezín was a transit camp, a way station between Jewish life as it had been in normal times,
and what now awaited the Jews of occupied Europe: slave labor and death.
Trains ran into Terezín and they carried people away to a number of locations, including Auschwitz-Birkenau, one hour from the Czech border town
of Ostrava. It was in Auschwitz-Birkenau that the Germans established a
special family camp for deportees from Terezín in September 1943, and
Schächter's choristers ended up there. The Jews in this family camp were
held as evidence against reports of mass murder. Specially privileged, these
inmates were spared the customary selection process, they wore their own
clothes, and they were not assigned to slave labor squads. During the first
days of March 1944, the Germans ordered them to write postcards to relatives, to prove their safe arrival in the east. The cards were dated March 25,
but the Jews who had written them had been killed on March 7. They had
served their purpose.

After their murder, another diplomatic problem arose for the Germans. Foreign diplomats and international welfare organizations began to ask slightly
more pointed questions about the fate of the Jews under German rule. In
response to deteriorating foreign relations, the Germans permitted a delegation of the International Red Cross to visit Theresienstadt on 23 June 1944.
It was the only Holocaust camp outside observers ever entered and, when it
came to it, it was not much of a delegation. The entire company comprised
three people: two Danes representing the Foreign Office and the Ministry

of Health, and one Swiss, the deputy head of the International Red Cross
(who came in place of his superior, who said he had to make another trip
just then). The Swedish Embassy was invited to send a representative but
declined because the visit conflicted with a national holiday.[29] Anticipating questions from the delegation about deportation, the Germans had dispatched two more transports, Schächter's choristers among them, to refill
the family camp in Birkenau. If worse came to worst, and a visit to Birkenau
were demanded, a group of deportees from Theresienstadt was on hand.

No such demand was made, no difficult questions were asked. By July 1944
it was clear to the Germans that this second lot of Jews in the family camp
would not be needed either. The family camp was dismantled; those found
"unfit for work" were gassed and the rest were sent on to slave labor sites.

Schächter's last ensemble entertained the International Red Cross delegation in Terezín in June 1944. "We heard ahead of time," Mariánka averred,
"not that we would have to sing *The Requiem* when they come. No. But that
we will have to be prepared to put on any performance they want, because
this is not only going to be some Nazi so-called dignitaries in their uniform,
but also some international people, maybe somebody from Switzerland,
maybe somebody from the International Red Cross." One wonders what the
visitors made of the exhausted, emaciated Jewish prisoners passionately
singing, "*Libera me, Domine, de morte aeterna.*" Deliver me, O Lord, from
eternal death.

The inmates were not delivered. But *The Requiem* delivered Mariánka from
the death of her soul. "I couldn't say that the music was always protecting
me, but I know that music saved my sanity. Whatever is safe, whatever is
still human, is not based on any religious belief. . . . but on living music."
The experience of singing with others gave her the sense of belonging that
Dr. Rosenfeld had introduced years before. "Dr. Rosenfeld made a family out of us, and during the war and after the war we adopted each other
as family members. We lost our families, most of us. Most of us lost every-

body. And the family that is alive today is the family that Rafi created. Rafi created a new family for us. We are brothers and sisters, and the few of us who are still alive are very fond of each other, and are also very forgiving about the negative parts of our personalities."

*   *   *

Few of Schächter's singers survived. The Germans ordered three transports in September and nine in October, for a total of 18,442 people. The ghetto population dwindled to 11,068. Little remained of the Terezín to which Mariánka was so deeply attached. But she had a physical remembrance of many she held dear. A lawyer named Ernst Wald gave Mariánka a stack of office paper. "Each a little bit different in color, a little yellowish or all white." In Terezín, "this was a treasure." To get the most out of it, Mariánka "folded it four times, you had four small pages." She did not stop there. "I took this paper to my factory. I showed it to Löwenstern. . . . I said, 'Löwenstern, *Können Sie mir ein Buch machen aus dem?* Can you make me a book out of this?" Although doing so meant that Löwenstern would have to pilfer materials, and although in any case this was a forbidden and therefore dangerous enterprise, he did not hesitate. "He said, 'We just take a little from them, and we use that for us. It's not going to last forever, but I'll make you a book; I am a bookbinder!" This was Mariánka's *Poesiealbum.* The European version of what Americans call an autograph album, this type of little notebook was coveted and treasured by young women and girls at the time. The first entry was written by Mariánka's mother. The second is by "Emil Löwenstern; Master Bookbinder, Krefeld, at present Theresienstadt." It is dated 16 September 1944.

Mariánka carried her *Poesiealbum* in her pocket. "Having the book with me—not always, but very often—usually after work hours I ran into people and I asked, 'Would you sign this for me?'" Some just wrote their signatures and, as she put it, "I have no idea who this is." But she quickly decided that, as the daughter of two artists, she should have "other painters and other artists and poets and musicians write in this." Carrying the album became increasingly important—sometimes because of a lucky encounter, and sometimes because of a tragic twist of fate. "I sometimes gave the book to somebody who signed it who was in the next transport. This happened with [the opera singer] Walter Windholz. One day he signed it; the next transport he was in it and I helped him with his packing."

Mariánka volunteered for extra work after the autumn 1944 deportations. "When the first transport left of people who were like my own family, I couldn't sleep anyway." The man who lit the heating stoves in the factory where she worked was deported and the woman who cleaned the two toilets died, and Mariánka offered to take over their tasks. With a pass in hand that allowed her to leave the camp alone at night, she walked to the factory. "I started my work at 3:00 a.m. to get the stoves going." She emptied them of ash, started the fires, swept the floors, and cleaned the toilets. "After I did the heating and cleaning the barracks, it was only 7:00 or 8:00 in the morning, so I stayed to help anybody who was slow in their work. At 3:00 [in the afternoon] I went home." Desolate as she was, she did not abandon music, nor did music abandon her. A number of musicians from the Amsterdam Concertgebouw orchestra remained in Terezín. "In the late afternoon they had rehearsal, and I would sit there. . . . I wanted more music. Yes."

Why was Mariánka spared? "Clerical error, no question about it. . . . Absolutely. The last transport, nearly all my friends left. The last one to the east, October 28, 1944, all the young people, the artists who had not been deported a week or two before, they left with that last transport." Nor did she succumb to the disease and hunger that ravaged the inmates who remained in the camp. Half a year later, Mariánka was there to welcome and to help Jews forced by the Germans to march west in advance of the Soviet army. In a grotesque reversal of the earlier transports, the Germans marched starving survivors of eastern death and labor camps back into transit camps such as Teresienstadt. "Day after day, people from the hunger marches came," her friend the tenor David Grünfeld among them.

The Germans fled Terezín at the end of April and the International Red Cross took the camp under its protection. When they were strong enough, Mariánka and her mother returned to Prague. She had her *Poesiealbum* with her.

*   *   *

It would be comforting to believe that now all was well. Or at least as well as it could be for Mariánka and her mother without Arnold. The Allies had won the war; Hilda and Mariánka were free. "*Libera me*," Mariánka had sung with Schächter's chorus. And now she was liberated.

But Mariánka and her mother returned to little: family, Jewish community, national identity—all destroyed, gone forever. For years Mariánka had dreamed of liberation, but what she experienced had nothing in common with those fantasies. "I was very close to suicide in 1945. The war was ended. In Prague. Where you saw nothing but empty windows of people who were dead." She inhabited a kind of no-man's-land. "At that time, I was nothing. I was not a citizen." Food was still rationed, and Mariánka "had German ration cards, which then meant Nazis." Scorned for her German birth, she was also the object of suspicion simply because she was alive. "[People] asked me, 'Did you help them in order to survive? How come you made it?'"

Mariánka asked for help at the Jewish community offices in Prague to change her legal status. In her memory, the officials were too few and too frightened to do anything for her. Overwhelmed by survivors' needs, or traumatized from their own experiences and loath to confront the Czech authorities about the question of national identity, they shrank from helping her. Ultimately Mariánka herself obtained "normal ration cards," and "Dr. Weinberg and Dr. Zimmer, who at first refused to help me, [asked], 'Would you consider helping us here?'" She accepted. "I needed an employment of some kind, even a barely paid one." For two years, from October 1945 until she immigrated to the United States in 1947, Mariánka worked in the legal department of the Jewish Community Center in Prague. She did general

office work, and she served as a translator and support for transient Jews in Prague who wanted to move on but did not have exit visas. Mariánka helped them negotiate the numerous government offices and forms required to obtain the papers they needed. "I loved it. I loved what I did there."

She also enjoyed seeing friends from Terezín, Schächter singers like Alice and Trudy Bondyová, in Prague. Karel Berman, Alexander Singer, and David Grünfeld lived together in an apartment just around the corner from her. Quite a number of the entries in Mariánka's *Poesiealbum* written by Terezín survivors date from the postwar Prague years. And she made new friends, especially among young Zionists who looked forward to establishing a Jewish state. Her plan at the time was to obtain an education and immigrate to Israel.

Neither worked out. Hilda, who was not a Zionist, ended up first in Italy and then in Israel, while Mariánka left for the United States.[30] This two-year period was the only time in their lives that they were separated. And Mariánka never got an education, not in Czechoslovakia and not in America. "I wanted help just to go to high school and have a diploma. There was no such thing. I never had another chance for schooling." She brought her mother to the United States; she married; she had two daughters. All of these enriched her life. But the Holocaust had reshaped her life permanently. "Some of us know that under other circumstances we would have done better. . . . I was interested in the medical field. I might have become a nurse practitioner or a researcher in a laboratory. And I definitely would have had to do with people." She and her husband had a chicken farm. "I had to do with nothing but chickens. For seventeen years, no people, never. Seven days a week. Later, five days a week. On the other two days, I tried to become a human being again, or write to people I had not seen in decades." After they sold the farm in 1969, Mariánka, the person who had lit the fires and cleaned the toilets in the *Galanteriewarenerzeugun* (the notions workshop) in Terezín, became a custodian in the public schools. "And the next eleven years, I had again no people because I was cleaning classrooms and bathrooms and throwing away garbage and having absolutely nothing to do with people."

Indeed, the Germans, their allies, and the paucity of immediate postwar help for survivors had ensured that Mariánka never achieved her potential. At the same time, Rafael Schächter and the musical world in which she participated in Terezín had shielded the flame of her humanity. "Many times in my life, I said to myself, 'I may have been killed by a bomb anywhere. In England [if I had gone on the *Kindertransport*] I may have survived. But I would only be half of who I am because I would not have met these musicians, the whole group of them, and our guiding light Rafael Schächter in the middle."

Notes

1. This and all subsequent quotations from Marianne Zadikow May are taken from oral histories conducted in New Paltz, New York, in 2000 and 2002 and telephone conversations in 2007.

2. Kurt Jakob Ball-Kadurie, *Das Leben der Juden im Deutschland in Jahre 1933: Ein Zeitbeicht* (Frankfurt-am-Main: Europaische Verlangstalt, 1963), 212.

3. Quoted in Kurt Jakob Ball-Kadurie, *Vor der Katastrophe: Juden in Deutschland* (Tel Aviv: Olamenu, 1967), 42.

4. Quoted in Vojtech Mastny, *The Czechs Under German Rule: The Failure of National Resistance* (New York and London: Columbia University Press, 1971), 21.

5. See Debórah Dwork and Robert Jan van Pelt, *Holocaust: A History* (New York: W. W. Norton, 2002), 135–45.

6. United States Department of State, *Documents on German Foreign Policy, 1918–1945*, Series D, 12 vols. (Washington, DC: U.S. Government Printing Office, 1949–62), vol.4, 270.

7. Zdenek Lederer, *Ghetto Theresienstadt* (London: Edward Goldston & Son, 1953), 13–14.

8. Raul Hilberg, *The Destruction of the European Jews*, vol. 2 (New Haven, Yale University Press, 2003), 430*ff*.

9. Lederer, *Ghetto Theresienstadt*, 14–15.

10. Ruth Bondy, *"Elder of the Jews": Jakob Edelstein of Thereisenstadt* (New York: Grove Press, 1989), 252–65.

11. Lederer, *Ghetto Theresienstadt*, 23, 247.

12. See Hilberg, *The Destruction of the European Jews*, vol.2, 430ff.; Lederer, *Ghetto Theresienstadt*, 8ff.; H. G. Adler, *Theresienstadt, 1941–1945: Das Antlitz einer Zwangsgemeinschaft* (Tubingen: J. C. B. Mohr [Paul Siebeck], 1960).

13. Adler, *Theresienstadt*, 47–48. See also Adler's extended discussion of these statistics on 37ff. Another note about the statistics of Terezín: A myth prevails that of the approximately 15,000 children deported to Theresienstadt, only 100 survived. This is not correct. According to Adler, 12,000 children were in Theresienstadt at one time or other. When the camp was liberated, there were 1,633 children under fifteen; another 100 of those who had been deported lived to see liberation (572–73). See also Debórah Dwork, *Children With A Star* (New Haven and London: Yale University Press, 1990), 295, n.22.

14. Bondy, *"Elder of the Jews,"* 291; Joža Karas, *Music in Terezín, 1941–1945* (New York: Beaufort Books, 1985), 11.

15. Adler, *Theresienstadt, 1941–1945*, 547–48, 560, 562; Council of Jewish Communities, *Terezín*, (Prague: Council of Jewish Communities in the Czech Lands, 1965), 78, 93; Lederer, *Ghetto Theresienstadt*, 41, 47, 97, 132–33, 137. Rabbi Leo Baeck was the last head of the *Jugendfuersorge*.

16. Unpublished diary of Otto Pollack, in the possession of his daughter, Helga Kinsky-Pollack, entry for 23 January 1943.

17. Oral history of Helga Kinsky-Pollack, conducted in Vienna, Austria, 15 August 1989.

18. Ibid.

19. Bondy, *"Elder of the Jews,"* 292; Karas, *Music in Terezín*, 15.

20. See Norbert Troller's discussion of the technical department, protection, and the artists' living conditions in his memoir *Theresienstadt: Hitler's Gift to the Jews* (Chapel Hill: University of North Carolina Press, 1991), 30–31, 93, 96.

21. For more on the *Lautschwerkstette*, see George Berkley, *Hitler's Gift: The Story*

of Theresienstadt (Boston: Branden Books, 1993), 133–34; and Bondy, *"Elder of the Jews,"* 347–48.

22. For more on working conditions, see Lederer, *Ghetto Theresienstadt*, 89–90.

23. Marianne Zadikow May, handwritten memoir, "How I Experienced the Holocaust"; letter from Ciba-Geigy to Ms. May, 3 April 1975.

24. For more on Hedda Grabová, see Karas, *Music in Terezín*, 15–19, 23ff. For more on transformation of the attics into living quarters, see Troller, *Theresienstadt*, 82.

25. Egon Redlich, *The Terezín Diary of Gonda Redlich*, ed. Saul S. Friedman (Lexington, KY: University Press of Kentucky, 1992), 86–87.

26. Quoted in Yitzhak Arad, *Ghetto in Flames: The Struggle and Destruction of the Jews in Vilna in the Holocaust* (New York: Holocaust Library, 1982), 321. See, too, the discussion of this issue in Dwork and van Pelt, *Holocaust: A History*, 220–27.

27. Kurt Singer, "Musikkritischer Brief Nr. 4: Verdis Requiem," in *Und die Musik spielt dazu: Chansons und Satiren aus dem KZ Theresienstadt*, Ulrike Migdal, ed. (Munich and Zurich: Piper, 1986), *170ff*.

28. Lederer, *Ghetto Theresienstadt*, 247; Redlich, *The Terezín Diary*, 129–30; Adler, *Theresienstadt, 1941–1945*, 697.

29. Jean-Claude Favez, *The Red Cross and the Holocaust* (Cambridge: Cambridge University Press, 1999), 43–45, 72–74. See also Lederer, *Ghetto Theresienstadt*, 116–20.

30. Hilda, who was born in Czechoslovakia, came under one quota for entry to the United States, whereas Mariánka, who was born in Germany, came under a more generous quota.

THE TEREZÍN ALBUM *of* MARIÁNKA ZADIKOW

I

Hab' Achtung vor dem Menschenbild.
Und denke daß, wie auch verborgen
Darin zu irgend einem Morgen,
der Keim zu allem Höchsten quillt.

Hab' Achtung vor dem Menschenbild.
Und denke daß, wie tief er stecke,
ein Hauch des Lebens der ihn wecke
Vielleicht aus deiner Seele quillt.

Respect the human being
And be mindful that, however deeply hidden,
Every morning
The germ for all that's highest swells therein.

Respect the human being
And be mindful that, however deep in him it may lie,
The wakening breath of life
May come from your soul.

Hilda Zadikow inaugurated her daughter's Poesiealbum *with two of the three stanzas of Friedrich Hebbel's (1813–1863) poem "Höechstes Gebot." Quoting from memory, Hilda's rendition differs little from Hebbel's original.*

Ick' leptung in dem Wunschwied
Und bücke doch, wie auch werhogen,
O aun zü irgend einen Worgen,
In kein zu allen zerzten —

Ick' leptung in dem Wunschwied
Und bücke doch, in lief er stecke,
In zauef der Leben die zu mehr
Vielleicht aus Oein Jule quillt

2

Im schönen Böhmerlande
Ist durch Zufall ein Gheto
entstanden. Hier sind
versammelt, verschiedenen
Nationen u. allen Branschen,
Künstler, Musiker Handwerker,
Arbeiter. Mit einfachen Mittel,
ohne jeden „Titel", soll das
Büch für fernere Zeiten Dir
stets in Erinnerung sein.

:: 16.IX.44
EMIL LÖWENSTERN
BUCHBINDERMEISTER
KREFELD, Z. ZT. THERESIENSTADT

In the beautiful Bohemian
land a ghetto came to be by
chance. Here are assembled
different nations and people
of all different occupations,
artists, musicians, craftsmen,
workers. With simple means,
without any "title," may this
book remain a memory for
you.

:: 09.16.44
EMIL LÖWENSTERN
MASTER BOOKBINDER
KREFELD, AT PRESENT THERESIENSTADT

Using materials filched from the notions workshop, the Galanteriewarenerzeugung, *Mariánka's co-worker, a bookbinder named Emil Löwenstern, created this* Poesiealbum.

Im schönen Böhmerlande
Ist durch Zufall ein
Ghetto entstanden.
Hier sind versammelt,
verschiednen Nationen
u. allen Branchen,
Künstler, Musiker
Handwerker, Arbeiter.
Mit einfachen Mittel
ohne jeden „Titel"
soll das Buch für
fernere Zeiten
Dir stets in Erinnerung
sein. 16. IX. 44.
Emil Löwenstern
Buchbindermeister
Krefeld. z. Zt. Theresienstadt.

3a

Was ist das Band, das sich um alle Herzen schlingt,	What is the bond encompassing all our hearts,
Das sie erobert in der ersten Stunde,	Conquering them within the very first hour,
Das süsse Ruh' in sie herniedersenkt,	Filling them with sweet peace at once
Sie wieder aufwühlt bis zum tiefsten Gründe?	Only to agitate them to the deepest depth?

Es ist ein Etwas, das wir alle kennen.   It is a Something known to all of us.
Weh' dem, der nie gefühlt die Wunderkraft!   Pity the one who never felt its wonders!
O' arme Toren, die ihr's nicht begreift,   Oh, you poor fools who never felt its powers,
Nur halbe Menschen können wir Euch nennen!   Only half-humans we can call you!

Ob's uns entgegentritt aus Menschenmunde,   Whether it comes to us through people's voices
ob schluchzend aus der Geige Töne quellen,   Or sobbing melodies from violins do swell
Heilend zu schliessen manche Herzenswunde,   Healing to soothe many a wounded heart

Was ist das Band, das sich um
            alle Herzen schlingt,
Das sie erobert in der ersten Stunde,
Das süsse Ruh' in sie horniedersenkt,
Sie wieder aufwühlt bis zum tiefsten
            Grunde?

Es ist ein Etwas, das wir alle kennen.
Weh' dem, der nie gefühlt die Wun=
            derkraft!
O'arme Toren, die ihr's nicht be=
            greift,
Nur halbe Menschen können wir
            Euch nennen!

Ob's uns entgegentritt aus
            Menschenmunde,
Ob schluchzend aus der Geige
            Töne quellen
Heilend zu schliessen manche
            Herzenswunde,

3ᵇ

Nie können wir ein Gleiches an die Seite stellen.
Der einen Kunst aus aller Künste Runde:
Musik—und ihrer holden Töne Wellen!

:: THERESIENSTADT, 21. SEPTEMBER 1944
ZUR ERINNERRUNG AN ERNST WALD

No other form of art can ever be compared
to the single one among arts' circle,
Music and all its gracious waves of tones

:: THERESIENSTADT, 21 SEPTEMBER 1944
AS A SOUVENIR OF ERNST WALD

Ernst (Arnošt in Czech) Wald (b. 29 June 1905) was a lawyer who participated in the intellectual life of Terezín as a lecturer. He surprised Mariánka with the gift of a "treasure": office paper that she tore into quarters and gave to Löwenstern to make this album. Wald was deported to Auschwitz on 16 October 1944 and was one of the prisoners brought back to Terezín as the war ended. Liberation thus found him there.

Nie können wir ein Gleiches an
die Seite stellen
Der einen Kunst aus aller Künste
Runde:
Musik – und ihrer holden Töne
Wellen!

Theresienstadt, 21. September 1944.

Zur Erinnerung an
Ernst Wald.

4

Zur Erinnerung an unsere in Theresienstadt begonnene Freundschaft
mit Dir unsern „Sonnenschein", in Liebe Deiner gedenkend,

:: VATER, MUTTI, U. LISE WALD

In memory of our friendship which began in Theresienstadt with
you, our "Sunshine," thinking of you with love,

:: FATHER, MOM, AND ILSE WALD

*Ilse Wald (or Waldová), born 22 October 1907, was deported to Terezín from Olomouc (Olmütz)
on 8 July 1942. She survived and was liberated in Terezín.*

Zur Erinnerung an unsere
in Theresienstadt begonnene
Freundschaft mit Dir unserm
„Sonnenschein", in Liebe
Deiner gedenkend,

Vater, Mutti u.

Ihr Wald.

5

Přeji Ti Marianko, skřivánku tu nejkrásnější písničku: Brzký
konec, návrat domu a ruky stisknutí k tomu.

:: WALDSTEIN KARLINSKÝ   I/XII 1944

I wish you, Mariánka, the bird's most beautiful song: A hasty end,
return home, and a firm handshake with it.

:: WALDSTEIN KARLINSKÝ   12.01.1944

*Waldstein Karlinský, an artist, lived in the same building at Jägergasse 9 as Mariánka and her
mother and many other artists.*

Přeji Ti Marianko, skřivánku
ku nejkrásnější písničku:
Brzký konec, návrat domu
a ruky stiskmuti k tomu.

Waldstein Karlinský

1/XII 1944

6

Marjánce! Skoro každý list Tvého památníčku obsahuje
vzpomínku na Terezín—Vzpomínejme raději na tu „neděli"
v Praze kdy jsme za zvuku Libušiných fanfár startovaly
Václavským náměstím, by jsme v Zemském museu myly sochy
a.t.d.—neníliž pravda . . . ?!

:: GULOVÝ OLGA   PRAHA, 20.9.45

For Marjánka! Nearly every page of our memory album contains
a memory of Terezín—We should rather remember that "Sunday"
in Prague when we started on Wenceslas Square accompanied
by the sound of the fanfares of the opera Libuše. We were on the
way to the National Museum in order to wash and clean statues,
etc.—Don't you think I am right . . . ?!

:: GULOVÝ OLGA   PRAGUE, 09.20.45

*Mariánka saw a number of Terezín survivors, Olga Gulový among them, in Prague after the war.
This entry dates from that period in her life.*

Marjánce!

Skoro každý list Tvého památníčku obsahuje vzpomínku na
Terezín, —

Vzpomínejme raději na tu
"neděli v Praze" kdy jsme so
"zvuku Libušiných fanfar
startovaly Václavským náměstím, by jsme v Zemském museu
myly schody a. t. d. —
nemíliž pravda....?!

Praha, 20. 9. 45

Julroj Olga

7

Nicht kann ich dichten wie Hans Wald. Noch wag' zu sprechen ich mit Euch über Musik. Nur denken mag ich, daß wir alle bald Geniessen mögen, neuer Freiheit Glück.

Der Zufall hat geführt uns hier zusammen aus fernen Gauen in die Stadt der Juden. Wir lernten kennen uns, so wie wir kamen, wie konnt es anders, die Schlechten und die Guten.

Doch hoffen wir, daß wir uns bald zerstreuen nach Nord und Süden, über Meer + Land, daß Ärger, Kummer, Not vergessen seien was bleibe, sei der Freundschaft fester Band.

:: MANFRED FÜRTH   THERESIENSTADT, 23. SEPT. 44

I am not able to rhyme as Hans Wald. Neither do I dare to speak with you about music. I only want to think that all of us will soon enjoy new freedom's joy.

Chance led us here together from faraway districts into the town of Jews. We met each other, just as we came, how else could it be, the bad ones and the good.

But let us hope that we may soon disperse to North and South over land and sea, that anger, sadness, want may be forgotten, remaining only friendship's solid bond!

:: MANFRED FÜRTH   THERESIENSTADT, 23 SEPT. 44

Manfred Fürth was deported to Terezín from the Netherlands. A German Jew, Fürth probably had sought refuge in Holland after Hitler came to power. Like Mariánka, he worked in the Galanteriewarenerzeugung (notions workshop), but in another room.

Nicht kann ich dichten wie Hans Wald
Noch wag' zu sprechen ich mit Euch
über Musik.
Nur denken mag ich, daß wir alle
bald
Geniessen mögen, neuer Freiheit Glück.

Der Zufall hat geführt uns hier
zusammen
Aus fernen Gauen in die Stadt der
Juden.
Wir lernten kennen uns, so wie
wir kamen,
Wie konnt es anders, die Schlechten
und die Guten.
Doch hoffen wir, daß wir uns bald zer-
streuen
Nach Nord und Süden, über Meer + Land
Daß Ärger, Kummer, Not vergessen
seien
Was bleibe, sei der Freundschaft festes
Band!

Manfred Firth

Theresienstadt 23. Sept. 44.

8

Das Glück ist eine flüchtige Welle,
Wer sich von ihr empor tragen lässt,
Weiss, das hinter ihr Das Tal liegt.

:: ZUM HERZLICHEN ANDENKEN AN DIETER
THS. 25.IX.44

Good luck is just a fleeting wave,
Whoever lets himself be carried upwards
Knows that behind it lies a valley.

:: IN CORDIAL REMEMBRANCE FROM DIETER
THS. 09.25.44

Dieter Langweil was born in Germany and sought refuge in Czechoslovakia after Hitler came to power. Mariánka and Dieter belonged to a group of young people who got together in Prague after the German occupation to make a "party" (they used the English word) from time to time. Dieter was deported to Terezín, and he and Mariánka saw each other a few times in the camp. He survived.

Das Glück ist eine
          flüchtige Welle,
Wer sich von ihr empor
          tragen lässt,
Weiss, das hinter ihr
          Das Tal lacht.

Zum herzlichen
Andenken
an
Dieter

Th. 25.IX.44.

9

Wenn ich einst—in besseren Tagen—an die in Theresienstadt
verbrachte Zeit zurückdenken werde, dann wird die Erinnerung
an meine liebenswürdige Arbeitskollegin „Mariánka" stets zu
den wenigen angenehmen Seiten dieses Aufenthaltes gehören.

:: JOSEF GRABSCHEID   THERESIENSTADT, 30. SEPT. 1944

When some day—in better times—I think back on the time I
spent in Theresienstadt, then the memory of my amiable work
colleague "Mariánka" will always belong to the few agreeable
parts of this residency.

:: JOSEF GRABSCHEID   THERESIENSTADT, 30 SEPT. 1944

*Josef Grabscheid (b. 29 May 1884) was transported from Olomouc (Olmütz) to Terezín on 8 July
1942. He survived and was liberated in Terezín.*

Wenn ich einst – in
besseren Tagen – an die in
Theresienstadt verbrachte
Zeit zurückdenken werde,
dann wird die Erinnerung
an meine liebenswürdige
Arbeits-Kollegin „Marianka"
stets zu den wenigen angenehmen Seiten dieses Aufent-
haltes gehören.

Josef Grabscheid

Theresienstadt, am 30. Sept. 1944.

IO

Na památku

:: DR. BEDŘICH ZIMMER   PRAHA, 24.10.45.

In memory

:: DR. BEDŘICH ZIMMER   PRAGUE, 10.24.45

After the war, Mariánka worked in the legal department of the Jewish Community Center in Prague, primarily for two people, the lawyers Dr. Bedřich Zimmer and Dr. Weinberg. Dr. Zimmer (b. 5 January 1911) was transported to Terezín from Prague on 4 February 1945 in a forced labor detail composed primarily of people who previously had been protected for one reason or another. He returned to Prague after liberation. Mariánka did general office work and helped transient Jews who couldn't speak Czech negotiate various official bureaus to obtain exit visas.

II

JAPANISCHE POESIE

Ein Skellet lacht, grinst—
Es erinnert sich des Lebens.

:: EUGEN   PRAHA, 19.X.45

JAPANESE POEM

A skeleton laughs, grins—
It remembers life.

:: EUGEN   PRAGUE, 10.19.45

Eugen Deitelbaum was picked up as a communist and survived five concentration camps. Mariánka met him after the war through her colleague in the law department of the Jewish Community Center, Marta Perotková, to whom he was engaged. He died in a drowning accident before they could be married.

Japanische Poesie.

Ein Skelett lacht, grinst —
Es erinnert sich des Lebens.

Eugen

Praha, 19. x. 45.

12

{ VERSO }   { RECTO }

Michael Angelo:
Dokonalost se zakládá na
maličkostech, ale dokonalost
není maličkost!!

:: MÉ MILÉ PARTNERCE KONCERTŮ
SULOVÁ   V PRAZE, 20.9.45

Mariánko!
Ruku Ti tisknu. S Bohem.
Na shledanou v lepších
časech.

:: TVŮJ STARÝ PŘÍTEL
TEREZÍN, 15.10.44   BALÁŽ JULA

Michaelangelo:
Perfection is based on trifles,
but perfection is no trifle!!

:: TO MY DEAR CONCERT PARTNER
SULOVÁ   IN PRAGUE, 09.20.45

Mariánka!
I press your hand. Go with God.
Till we meet again in better times.

:: YOUR OLD FRIEND JULA BALÁŽ
TEREZÍN, 10.15.44

Mariánka no longer recalls with certainty, but she believes she and Sulová sat together in the audience of a concert, applauding enthusiastically.

Jula Baláž (Julius Baláž), born 5 October 1901, wrote this entry the day before he was deported to Auschwitz. Of the 1,500 prisoners shipped out of Terezín on 16 October 1944, only 110 survived. Jula Baláž was not among them.

Mariánko!

Píšeme Ti lístken...

S Bohem. Na

shledanou v lepších

časech.

Trůj starý přítel

Terezín
15.10.44.

Michael Angelo:

Dokonalost se zakládá na maličkostech,
ale dokonalost není maličkost.!!

v Brně, 20.9.45   mě porková konverti

13

„Theresienstadt" jemals vergessen, heißt—fast ein—
Verbrechen—wie dieses!— :: C. MEINHARD 4. MAI 45

"Theresienstadt" ever to forget, that would be nearly as much a
crime as this one! :: C. MEINHARD 4 MAY 45

Carl Meinhard (also spelled Karl Meinhardt) and Rudolf Bernauer were important theater producers in Berlin before and after World War I. In 1910 the two men leased their own premises, the Berlin Theater on Charlottenstrasse. Meinhard's wide-ranging creative interests embraced the developing motion picture art form, and in 1932, at age fifty-seven, he produced a movie called Quick.

Meinhard was also known for his political voice. He was one of the signatories of a petition to change Paragraph 267 of the Weimar Republic Civil Law Code, which forbade specific homosexual practices. This petition became a cause célèbre and its signers were a who's who of German society at the time, including, for example, Albert Einstein and Thomas Mann.

Deported to Terezín, Meinhard joined the many other artists and musicians who continued to create and produce in the camp. He worked as stage director with composer Viktor Ullmann and singers Karel Berman (bass-baritone), David Grünfeld (tenor), Marion Podolier (soprano), and Hilde Aronson-Lindt (mezzo-soprano) on Ullmann's opera Der Kaiser von Atlantis. Banned by the Germans at the last minute, the opera was not performed for another thirty years. Ullmann and most of the singers in the production were deported to Auschwitz in October 1944; few survived. Meinhard was liberated in Terezín.

„Theresienstadt"
jemals ver-
gessen, heißt
— fast ein
— Verbrechen —
— wie dieses ! —

7. Mai 65

Carl Meinhard
— MEINHARD —

14

„Die Menschen lieben werden ist der einzige wahre Glück." (Platen)

:: DR. [*illegible*]   THERESIENSTADT, 11.5.45

"To love people is the only true happiness."

:: DR. [*illegible*]   THERESIENSTADT, 05.11.45

„Die Menschen lieben können
ist das einzige wahre Glück."
                                    (Platen)

Deine Mutti

Frankenthal, 11. 5. 45.

15

MARIANNE HAT FREIEN TAG!

:: H. Z.

Marianne has a day off!

:: H. Z.

A drawing by Mariánka's mother, Hilda Zadikow.

MARIANNE HAT
FREIEN TAG!

H·Z·

16

A rajskou krásou vzplane nebes tvář, že láskou k noci vzhoří celý
svět. . . . . . :: TVŮJ OBDIVOVATEL A KAMARÁD   JINDRA   PRAHA V PROSINCI 1945

And the beauty of paradise illuminates the sky as all the world is
aglow by its love for the night. . . . . :: YOUR ADMIRER AND FRIEND
JINDRA   PRAGUE IN DECEMBER 1945

Jindra was a good friend of Mariánka's after the war in Prague. He was not Jewish. His father, a lawyer, was reputed to have helped Jews, most particularly Jews who had married gentiles in what the Nazis called "mixed" marriages. Such couples sorely needed legal help, but few attorneys were willing to offer it.

A prajskou krásou
vzplane nebes tvář,
že báskou k noci
vzhoří celý svět......

Tvůj
    obdivovatel
    a kamarád

    Jindra

Praha • prosinci 1945.

17

Když Tě nikdo nepřeveze, my Tě převezem.
podle N.Ú.C.

:: ARNOŠT HANKE
MEZINÁRODÍ ZASILATELSTVÍ
PRAHA I—MASNÁ 8—TELEFON Č. [*illegible*]
V NÁRODNÍ SPRÁVĚ
ZDENĚK VÍTEK   RODEK RUDOLF   21.V.1946

If no one agrees to move you, we will move you.
according to the N.U.C.

:: ARNOŠT HANKE
INTERNATIONAL SHIPPING AGENTS
PRAGUE I—MASNA ST. 8—TEL. # [*illegible*]
IN NATIONAL MANAGEMENT
ZDENĚK VÍTEK   RODEK RUDOLF   05.21.1946

Rodek Rudolf got to England during the war, where he joined the Czech division of the Royal Air Force. He returned to Prague after the war, and Mariánka met him then. He worked for a moving company, hence the play on words.

Když Tě nikdo nepřeveze
my Tě převezem

podle N.Ú.C.

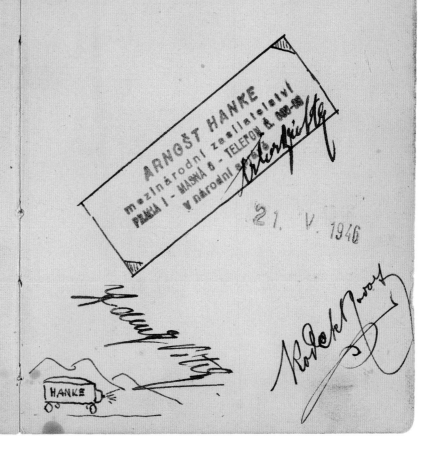

ARNOŠT HANKE
mezinárodní zasílatelství
PRAHA I - MASNÁ 6 - TELEFON Č. 648-66
v národní správě

21. V. 1946

HANKE

18

Theresienstadt, Oktober 1944
Es geht den Berg hinauf,
Es geht den Berg hinunter,
Wir bleiben unserm Glauben treu,
Und geh'n deshalb nicht unter.

:: DIAMANT

Theresienstadt, October 1944
It is going up the hill,
It is going downhill.
We remain true to our faith,
and therefore will not perish.

:: DIAMANT

The picture was drawn by Marianne Fröhlich (M. F.), who also inscribed the four lines below it. Mariánka's workshop boss signed his name, Diamant, in the lower right corner. Known as a mean-spirited fellow in Prague before the war, Diamant did not improve in Terezín. Mariánka remembers his wife as "a lovely woman." Frölich would inscribe another picture for Mariànka shortly after Terezín's liberation (see entry 105).

19

Viele Wege führen durch
den Wald, viele Wege
durch's Leben geh'n, wer
nicht Bescheid weiß, verirrt
sich bald!

Vielmals danke ich Dir,
für die unbewußt schönen
Stunden, die Du mir
manchmal geschenkt hast.

:: RUTH FÜRTHOVÁ

Many a path leads
through the forest, many paths
lead through life.
Those who are not in the know
may easily lose their way.

Many thanks
for the beautiful hours
which, unaware, you have
sometimes given to me.

:: RUTH FÜRTHOVÁ

Viele Wege führen durch
den Wald, viele Wege
durch's Leben geh'n. Wer
nicht Bescheid weiß, verirrt
sich bald!

Vielmals danke ich Dir,
für die unbewußt schönen
Stunden, die Du mir
manchmal geschenkt hast.
Ruth Türthova.

20

Denke offt und gerne
Dich in weiter ferne
an die Schuhl in der
Magdeburger Kasserne

:: ZU ERINNERUNG   DEIN SUSSMANN
6. JUNI 1945

Think often and gladly
even if you are far away
of the "schul" in the
Magdeburg Barracks.

:: IN MEMORY   YOUR SUSSMANN
6 JUNE 1945

In Mariánka's memory, Sussmann was a very religious man who was reputed to have been a rabbi before the war.

6. Juni 1945.

Denke stets und gerne
Auch in weiter Ferne
An die Schule
In der Magdeburger
Kaserne.

Zur Erinnerung
Dein Sussmann

2I

Marjánko,
jakkoli Vám bude, vždycky tyto řádky
považujte za srdečný stisk ruky,
připomínající usměvavou, čistou
sílu, o níž jsme spolu mluvívali.
„Vyhrajte svou hru!"
:: H. TARASZKA   H. TARASZKOVÁV   ZÁŘÍ 1947

Mariànka,
no matter how you should feel, always consider
these lines to be a heartfelt handshake
that recalls the cheerful, pure
force about which we used to talk.
"Win your game!"
:: H. TARASZKA   H. TARASZKOVÁ   SEPTEMBER 1947

P

Marjánko,

jakkoli Vám bude, vždycky tyto řádky
považujte za srdečný stisk ruky,
připomínající usměvavou, čistou
sílu, o níž jsme spolu mluvívali:

"Vyhrajte svou hru!"

V září 1947   *[podpis]*

M. Fanaszková

22

Mit vielen guten Wünschen

:: VON DEINER LILY FISCHL

TEREZÍN, 22.X.1944

With many good wishes

:: FROM YOUR LILY FISCHL

TEREZÍN, 10.22.1944

Born in Vienna in 1898, Lily Fischl fled to Prague with her husband and children, presumably after the Anschluss of Austria in March 1938. The children were sent to England, probably on a Kindertransport after the Germans invaded Czechoslovakia in March 1939. Lily Fischl and her husband were deported to Terezín in 1942, where Mr. Fischl died.

Mariánka remembers vividly what happened to Lily that October day in 1944 when the older woman signed her Poesiealbum. *By this time, Mariánka and her mother were situated in their third (and last) lodging. Lily "was*

one of my mother's students. She sat in our room that we had already. A good room with a nice window. It was ours. And the toilet we shared with I think only four other people. And as she sat there in 1944, in October—she sat there and started to paint very much in the way my mother taught her. I'm not quite sure which of the flowers are hers, because she got her transport slip and she had to leave immediately, and my mother finished it. [Note Hilda Zadikow's initials, bottom left.] Lily Fischl went to Auschwitz and returned. I heard from somebody who knew her in Auschwitz that she became everybody's mother in that block [barrack]. Lily was there

for everybody. To let them cry on her shoulder, or let them ask her questions, or just be with her, or whatever."

Lily's entry is dated 22 October 1944. The Germans dispatched a transport to Auschwitz the next day. Of the 1,715 Jews on that particular train, 159 survived, Lily among them. Shipped back to Terezín in the last weeks of the war, she was in the camp when it was liberated in 1945. A year later, Lily was reunited with her children in England.

The zinnias in this picture were drawn from memory. There were no zinnias in Terezín.

H.Z.

mit vielen guten Wünschen
von deiner Lilly Feigel.
Terezin, 22.X. 1944.

23

Milé Mariánce
v upomínku.

:: VĚRA A TUREK (SCHIFFOVI)
PRAHA, 16.X.47

For dear Mariánka
in memory.

:: VERA AND TUREK (SCHIFF)
PRAGUE, 10.16.47

Vera Schiff (b. 17 May 1926) and her family were deported to Terezín, where they suffered devastating loss: sister, parents, grandmother. She wrote about her experiences in her memoir, Theresienstadt: The Town the Nazis Gave to the Jews. *Vera signed Mariánka's* Poesiealbum *in Prague, when Mariánka, who had been educated to take care of newborns, came to give Vera and Turek's first baby his first bath.*

Milé Haničce

v upomínku.

Věra a Turek
(Schiffovi)

Praha, 16. II. 47.

24

Meine liebe Kleine! Mögen wir die schlimmsten Zeiten
ungetrennt überleben, und in den Guten weiter so innig
befreundet bleiben! :: DEINE MUTTER   TEREZÍN, DEN 28.X.1944

My dear little one! May we survive the bad times without being
separated and may we remain such heartfelt friends in good
times! :: YOUR MOTHER   TEREZÍN, 10.28.1944

*From Mariánka's birth until Hilda's death, mother and daughter were separated for only two
and a half years. After the war, Hilda, who was not a Zionist, went to the new state of Israel.
Mariánka, who wished to go to Israel, ended up in the United States. While the particulars
of their case are unusual, the principle is not. Jewish survivors of the Holocaust sought entry
into many countries simultaneously. All sorts of rules and exceptions applied in each petition,
including consideration of age, country of origin, occupation, and the like. When an opportunity
to immigrate materialized, few survivors postponed departure in hope of a better offer. The idea
was, "I'll take this, and then we'll see." And indeed, once in the United States, Mariánka soon set
in motion the paperwork that would enable her mother to join her.*

Meine liebe Kleine! Mögen wir
die schlimmen Zeiten ungetrennt
überstehen, und in den guten
weiter so innig befreundet
bleiben!
                    Deine Mutter.

Terezín, d. 28.X. 1944.

25

V upomínku na poslední uplakanou „Studni" v Terezíně.

:: KAREL URBA

JIRKA GOLDSCHMIED

[*illegible*]

KOLÍNKÝ FRANTA

WEINSTEIN M.

FIŠHL JIŘI

HONZA JÍLOVSKÝ

[*illegible*]

JIRKA LEDERER

In memory of the last touching "In the Well" in Terezín.

:: [SIGNATURES AS ABOVE]

These twelve signatories were choristers in the one-act comic opera In the Well *by Czech composer Vilém Blodek (1834–1874). Mounted by Karel Berman (entry 34 verso) in his first attempt at opera conducting,* In the Well *was shut down by a German order demanding that all public performances be in German. In Mariánka's memory, the production never premiered and the inscription refers to the last rehearsal. According to Joža Karas, however, the order was given on a Monday but did not take effect until Thursday, so* In the Well *was performed once, on Wednesday night. (Joža Karas,* Music in Terezín, 1941–1945 *[New York: Beaufort Books, 1985], 32.) Karel Berman returned to his rendition of* In the Well *after the war.*

V upomínku na poslední
uplakanou „Studni " v Terezíně.

Paul Triba,
Mike Goldschmid

[signatures illegible]

Kolínský pacuto Weinstein [?]

[signatures illegible]

26

{ VERSO }

{ RECTO }

Moje barva červená a bílá,
moje heslo, poctivost a síla!

:: LEDERER HONZA   FRANK WALTER
[*illegible*]

:: V TĚŽKÉ DOBĚ NAPSALA TVÁ
PŘÍTELKYNĚ HERTA   21.X.1942 V TEREZÍNĚ

:: LEDERER HONZA   FRANK WALTER
[*illegible*]

My colors are red and white,
my slogan, honesty and strength!

:: WRITTEN IN DIFFICULT TIMES BY YOUR
FRIEND HERTA   10.21.1942 TEREZÍN

This entry is dated 21 October 1942. Either the date is wrong or this sheet was bound into the album when Emil Löwenstern made this notebook for Mariánka in September 1944 (see entry 2).

Lederer Honza
Frank Walter
Müller

21.X.1942 v Teresieně.

Moje barva,
    červená a bílá,
moje heslo,
    poctivost a síla!
V těžké době
napsala Tvá
    přítelkyně Hertha

27

Lieve Mariánka

Als ik een dichters geest bezat,
Dan zou ik op dit albumblad
Een heel mooi versje schrijven
Maar daar ik deze gave mis
Wens ik alleen wat nodig is
Een recht gelukkig leven.

:: JE UBIKATION GENOOT,
ELISABETH WACHSBERG

Dear Mariánka

If I had the mind of a poet,
I would write a beautiful poem for you
on this sheet in your album.
But as I lack this gift
I can only wish you what is most needed:
A very happy life.

:: YOUR BARRACK COMRADE,
ELISABETH WACHSBERG

Deported to Terezín from the Netherlands, eleven-year-old Elisabeth Wachsberg did not paint the Bohemian hills she saw around her; instead, she drew upon her memory to create this typical Dutch landscape. She survived the war.

Lieve Marianka.

Als ik een dichtergeest bezat,
Dan zou ik op dit albumblad
Een heel mooi versje schrijven
Maar daar ik deze gave mis
Wens ik alleen wat nodig is
Een recht gelukkig leven.
ye Akikation genoot
Elisabeth
Wachsberg.

E. Wachsberg

28

Milé Mariance na památku na slavné časy Terezínské

:: W. WINDHOLZ 25.IX.44

To dear Mariánka to remember the famous times in Terezín

:: W. WINDHOLZ 09.25.44

Walter Windholz (b. 1 September 1907) was deported to Terezín from Klatovy on 26 November 1942. A baritone, he sang in many Terezín productions, including The Bartered Bride, *conducted by Rafael Schächter;* Carmen, *conducted by Franz Eugen Klein; and concerts featuring a range of composers from Mahler to Smetana to Terezín composers Viktor Ullmann and Hans Krasa. Windholz was deported to Auschwitz on 16 October 1944, just a few weeks after he had signed Mariánka's album. He did not survive.*

Milé Marrauce na
památku na slavné
časy Terezínské

[signature]

25. X. 44

29

Nikdy nemohu zapomenouti na Tvé přátelství, které mne potěšilo a sílilo v době, kdy mně bylo nejhůře. Věřím, že i v dobrých dobách na sebe nezapomeneme.

:: TVOJE MARTA TAMARA ZUCKEROVÁ
9.10.44

Never will I be able to forget your friendship which gave me solace and strength in a time when I felt the worst. I believe that also in good times we shall not forget each other.

:: MARTA TAMARA ZUCKEROVÁ
10.09.44

Marta Tamara Zuckerová (b. 4 November 1900) was transported from Prague to Terezín on 24 October 1942. Almost precisely two years later, on 23 October 1944, she was sent to Auschwitz, where she perished.

Nikdy nemohu zapomenouti
na tvé přátelství, které
mne potěšilo a sílilo
v době, kdy mně bylo
nejhůře.
Věřím, že i v dobrých
dobách na sebe nezapomeneme.

Tvoje
Marte Tamara –
Zuckerová.

9/10. 44.

30

Na památku na zdejší působení
své milé Mariance

:: TVŮJ VĚRNÝ PŘÍTEL ROBERT DUB
V TEREZÍNĚ DNE 20. ŘÍJNA 1944 DVA DNI
PŘED ODJEZDEM DO NEZNÁMA.

In memory of this field
of work to my dear Mariánka

:: YOUR FAITHFUL FRIEND ROBERT DUB
IN TEREZÍN, ON THE 20TH OF OCTOBER 1944
TWO DAYS BEFORE DEPARTURE INTO THE
UNKNOWN.

Robert Dub was deported to Auschwitz three days after he wrote this entry. It is believed he was born 20 December 1928, was deported from Prague to Terezín on 6 March 1943, and was liberated in Friedland, a subcamp of Gross-Rosen.

Na památku na
zdejší působení
své milé Marjánce

Tvůj věrný
přítel
Robert Stein

V Terezíně dne 20. října 1944
Dva dni před odjezdem
do neznáma.

3I

Die Welt ist so offen	The world is so open
die Welt ist so weit	The world is so wide
wann kommt sie, wann kommt sie	When will it reach us
die herrliche Zeit?	That glorious time?
Es ist nur die Frage	The question is only
wann und wie?	When and however?
Sind es nur Tage	Just days from now
Wird es nie?	Or might it be never?
Wir warten und harren	We are patiently waiting
und leben dahin	Just living along
die Stunden, sie rinnen	The hours escaping
die Tage, sie flieh'n.	The days are soon gone.
Die Zeit, sie entschwindet	The time disappearing
die Zeit lauft so schnell	As days change into night
wers überwindet?	Which of us will subdue it?
wann wirds es hell?	When will there be light?

Die Welt ist so offen
die Welt ist so weit
wann kommt sie, wann komt sie
die herrliche Zeit?

Es ist nur die Frage
wann und wie?
sind es nur Tage
wird es nie?

Wir warten und harren
und leben dahin
die Stunden, sie rinnen
die Tage, sie flieh'n.

Die Zeit, sie entschwindet
die Zeit lauft so schnell
wers überwindet?
wann wird es hell?

32

Die Sonne der Freiheit
lass' uns erleben
das ist wohl das Einzigste
ersehntestes Streben.
Dies mein Wunsch für alle
unsere Glaubensgenossen
zum Gedenken an Ihre

:: KOLLEGIN HELLA GIBIAN
25.X.1944

Let us live to experience
Freedom's delight
The only thing worth
our struggle and strife.
This is my wish for all
our fellow-believers
In memory of your

:: COLLEAGUE HELLA GIBIAN
10.25.1944

Hella Gibian (Helena Gibiánová), born 22 September 1893, was transported to Terezín from Prague on 20 June 1942. She survived in Terezín.

Die Wonne der Freiheit
lass' uns erleben,
das ist wohl das Einzigste
ersehntestes Streben.

Dies mein Wunsch für Alle
unsere Glaubensgenossen
zum Gedenken an Ihre
Kollegin Sella Gibian.

25. X. 1944.

33

Es schwinden jedes Kummers Falten, solang' des Liedes Zauber
walten. Dies soll in Ihrem Leben immer sein. Ihre Ihnen zugetan

:: SOPHIE KLINKE   THERESIENSTADT, 7.X. 44

All the wrinkles of sadness vanish while the song's magic
remains. Thus it should always be in your life. Your devoted

:: SOPHIE KLINKE   THERESIENSTADT, 10.07.44

Sophie (possibly Josefa) Klinke played the role of Mařenka in The Bartered Bride. *Mariánka
saw this production before she joined the Schächter chorus; Sophie had, she said, a beautiful
soprano voice. Called up for deportation, Sophie happened to see Mariánka two days before her
forced departure on 9 October 1944. She wrote this entry by way of farewell. Sophie was sent to
Auschwitz. She survived.*

Es schwinden jedes Kum-
mers Falten, solang
des Liedes Zauber
walten.

 Dies soll in Ihrem
Leben immer sein,
  Ihre Ihnen zuge-
tane
   Sophie Münke.
Theresienstadt, 7.X.44.

34

Marjánce, aby byla vždycky
tak hodná.

:: K. BERMAN

24/9 1944

For Mariánka, may you always
be this kind.

:: K. BERMAN

09.24.1944

O.Scheinpflugová
Otče náš jenž jsi na nebesích
posvět' se jméno Tvé,
jenž jsi stvořil bolest, kterou láskou zveme.
Pláčeme a přece děkujeme Tobě.
A tobě taky, chlapče s černýma očima.

:: TEREZÍN, 31.X.1944

VÍM, ŽE NIKDY NEZAPOMENEŠ,

PROČ JSEM TI TO NAPSALA.

YOUR NINA

O. Scheinpflugová
Our Father who art in heaven,
hallowed be Thy name.
You who hast created the pain we call love.
We weep and yet we thank thee.
And also you, young man with black eyes.

:: TEREZÍN, 10.31.1944

I KNOW THAT YOU WILL NEVER FORGET

WHY I WROTE THIS TO YOU.

YOUR NINA

Bass-baritone Karel Berman (1919–1995) and Mariánka were great friends in Terezín. Deported from Prague to the Lípa camp on 16 January 1942, Berman was one of 120 men pulled out of that camp and sent, via Prague, on the Cv transport to Terezín (6 March 1943). Berman worked as a corpse carrier during the day and performed in musical productions in the evening (see entries 25–26). He was shipped to Auschwitz on 28 September 1944. He survived and was liberated in Allach. Karel and Mariánka continued to see each other when they returned to Prague after the war; Karel, Alexander Singer (entry 48), and David Grünfeld (entry 49 recto) lived in

Bela Feldman's "beautiful, huge apartment" just around the corner from Mariánka. After Mariánka immigrated to the United States, Berman visited her in 1971. He remained in Czechoslovakia after the war, attended the Prague Conservatory, and had an illustrious career as an opera singer, stage director, and member of the Czech National Theater in Prague.

Nina Schwarz (also called Schwarzová) voluntarily converted to Catholicism when she was a young girl. Mariánka met Nina in Terezín, and the devout Catholic, a few years older than

she, became her confidante. They gave each other affection and moral support, and they sang together in Schächter's chorus. When the maestro decided to put on Verdi's Requiem, Nina lent him her missal so he could study the prayers. After the war, Nina returned to Prague. By the time Mariánka left Czechoslovakia in 1947, Nina was on her way to becoming a Carmelite nun. The two remained in correspondence. They saw each other again in 1995, visiting in Prague and traveling together with Mariánka's closest childhood friend, Ruth Bratu (née Theiner), to see Terezín once more.

Maryšce (aby byla šťastná
tak hodná ......
24/8 1944

O. Scheinpflugová.

Otče náš jenž jsi na nebesích

posvěť se jméno Tvé,

jenž jsi stvořil bolest, kterou láskou zveme.

Pláčeme a přece děkujeme Tobě.

A tobě taky, chlapče s černýma očima.

Terezín 31. X. 1944.

Vím, že nikdy nezapomeneš,
proč jsem Ti to napsala.

Tvá Nina.

35

Im Munde die Warhheit,
Im Auge die Treu'
Im Herzen die Liebe,
Bewahre die Drei.
Liebes Mariandl,
ich kann weder dichten, noch zeichnen,
bin ganz untalentiert, ich wünsche
Ihnen für Ihre weitere Zukunft, das
alles, allerbeste und denken Sie auch
hin und da
an Ihre

:: HILDE SCHLESINGER
PRAG, DEN 28.1.1946

In your mouth truth
In your eye faithfulness
In your heart Love
Preserve these three.
Dear Mariandl,
I can neither rhyme nor draw
am totally without any talent
I wish for you and your further
future the very very best and
do think once in a while
of your

:: HILDE SCHLESINGER
PRAGUE, 01.28.1946

Like many other Terezín inmates, Mariánka was incarcerated in the camp prison for a minor infraction of one of the numerous rules and directives—or for no reason at all. Hilde (or Hilda) Schlesinger was one of the women with whom Mariánka shared a cell in autumn 1942. Schlesinger (b. 9 November 1900)was deported from Prague to Terezín on 12 February 1942. She was sent on to Auschwitz that December, possibly as a consequence of incarceration in Terezín. Astonishingly, she survived, and was liberated in Bergen-Belsen. Hilde Schlesinger returned to Prague.

Im Munde die Wahrheit,
Im Auge die Treu'
Im Herzen die Liebe,
Bewahre die Drei.

Liebes Mariandl,

ich kann weder dichten, noch zeichnen
bin ganz untalentiert, ich wünsche
Ihnen für Ihre weitere Zukunft, das
alles, allerbeste und denken Sie auch
hie und da

un Ihre
Hilde Schlesinger

Prag, am 28./I. 1946

36

Transport není žádná sranda kavárna byla lepší

:: FRANTA   24.9.44

Transport is no joke the coffeehouse was better

:: FRANTA (STRÁNSKÝ)   09.24.44

Franta Stránský (b. 3 July 1909) was deported to Auschwitz a few days after he wrote this entry. The coffeehouse he mentions refers to Rafael Schächter and Eda Krása's (entry 39) living quarters, where friends sometimes met after working hours. He did not survive.

Transport není
žádná pravda
kovárna byla lepší

Franta

24.9.44.

37

Liebe Marianne,
Es gibt viele Juden in Terezín. Man weist nicht woher und man
weist nicht wohin. Man sieht sie, kommen man sieht sie gehen.
Aber unsere Freundschaft bleibt immer bestehen.

:: ANNY MORPURGO

Dear Marianne,
There are many Jews in Terezín. One does not know where they
came from and one does not know where they are going.
One sees them arriving, one sees them go away. But our
friendship is here to stay.

:: ANNY MORPURGO

*Deported to Terezín from the Netherlands, Anny Morpurgo was eleven when she wrote and
drew this entry. Although her father was an artist, she took drawing lessons from Hilda Zadikow.
Anny and her father were quartered in the same as house at Jägergasse 9 as Mariánka and Hilda.
Both father and daughter survived.*

Liebe Marianne

Es gibt viele Juden in Terezin.
Man weiss nicht woher und man
weist nicht wohin.
Man sieht sie, kommen man sieht
sie gehen.
Aber unsere Freundschaft bleibt
immer bestehen.

Anny Morpurgo

38

Zur freundlicher Erinnerung.

:: [*illegible*]   27.I.1946

For a friendly memory

:: [*illegible*]   01.27.1946

According to Mariánka, this person came to see her when she worked at the Jewish Community Center in Prague. The signature is illegible, and she does not remember who it was.

Zur freundlichen Er-
innerung.

27/I. 1946

39

Lev je králem zvířat, to Ti přeje

:: TVŮJ EDA.   TH. 24.IX.1944 O PŮLNOCI.

Lion is the king of all animals, this is the wish of

:: YOUR EDA   TH. 11.24.1944 AT MIDNIGHT

Eda (Edgar) Krása (b. 1924) was deported to Terezín on 24 November 1941 with the first Aufbaukommando (construction crew). After building the kitchens in Terezín, he worked as a cook by day and sang in Rafael Schächter's chorus during his "free" time. A close friend of Mariánka, Krása also knew Schächter very well indeed: he shared an unheated, bug-infested attic room with the maestro for three years. Leo Haas, one of the artists assigned to the technical department, painted three portraits (which still exist today) of Krása in Terezín. Krása, Schächter, and Haas were deported to Auschwitz in October 1944. Haas and Krása survived. Krása was liberated in Blechhammer, an Auschwitz subcamp. He lives in Newton, Massachusetts.

Lev je krásné zvíře,
to Ti přeje
Tvůj Eda

Th. 24. IX. 1944.
o půlnoci.

40

Dutch artist Josef (Jo) Spier (1906–1978) was well known as an illustrator and cartoonist before the war. His love for the Netherlands was reflected in his art and, in return, the Dutch public loved him. In 1938 his countrymen voted him one of the ten most popular living Dutchmen. Shielded from the Germans by Dutch bureaucrats (perhaps including prominent Dutch Nazis), Spier and his family were sent to the town of Doetinchem and sheltered in a villa, under house arrest, while the deportations raged. This protection ended in April 1943 and

the Spier family was deported to Terezín. Assigned to the technical department as an artist, he also worked with Hilda Zadikow in the Lautsch company workshops and was the set designer for the Nazi propaganda film Theresienstadt: A Documentary from the Jewish Settlement Area. *The Spier family survived and returned to the Netherlands after the war. It was not a happy situation. Spier's countrymen, both gentile and Jewish, could not fathom why he had been accorded special treatment. Rumors flew of collaboration with the Germans. Disheartened, Spier and*

his family immigrated to the United States in 1951, where their friendship with Hilda continued with visits to her home in Pine Bush, New York.

Spier wrote an illustrated book about his experiences in Terezín: Dat alles heeft mijn oog gezien *[My Eyes Saw It All].*

lo Spien.

4I

Zum Andenken an Seine einzige „Verwandte" (Vaše kráva pila
naše mléko!) Alles Gute für die Zukunft, Cousinchen!

:: LOTTE   5.V.45

In memory of your only "relative" (your cow drank our milk!)
All the very best for the future, little cousin!

:: LOTTE   05.05.45

Lotte's mother and Hilda Zadikow's cousin were sisters-in-law.

Zum Andenken an
Deine einzige
Verwandte. (vaše
"kráva pila naše
mléko.")
Alles Gute für
die Zukunft,
Cousinchen!

Lotte

5. V. 45.

42

V upomínku na „Humoresku"

:: [*illegible*]   13.4.45.

In memory of "Humoresque"

:: [*illegible*]   04.13.45

This bit of Dvořák's Humoresque *(op. 101, no. 7) was inscribed by a Czech violinist at Mariánka's request after a concert.*

О промитки на
„Нимфетки"

13/4. 45.

43

Mit herzlichen Dank für den tschechischen Unterricht und zur
freundlichen Erinnerung an den Wachmann der Südbaracken.

:: PAUL KRONHEIM   TERESÍN 20.4.45

With heartfelt thanks for the Czech lessons and in friendly
memory of the guard of the South Barracks.

:: PAUL KRONHEIM   TEREZÍN 04.20.45

*Paul Kronheim was an inmate of Terezín. His job was to guard the South Barracks, which
housed a factory.*

Mit herzlichem
Dank für den
bachischen Unterricht
und zur freundlichen
Erinnerung an den
Wachmann der
Süd Baracken;

Teresín 20.4.45

44

Mit herzlichen grusse von einem der Hollandischen geiger mit dem wunsch Ihnen in gesundheit wieder zu sehen.

:: SIEGFRIED DE BOER

With cordial greetings from one of the Dutch violinists who wishes to meet you again in good health.

:: SIEGFRIED DE BOER

Siegfried de Boer had been a violinist in the Amsterdam Concertgebouw orchestra.

Mit herzlichen Gruss.
von einem der Holl.
 landischer geiger
mit dem wunsch
Ihnen in gesund..
heit wieder zu
sehen

Siegfried Boen

45

Na Terezín co nejméně vzpomínej, ale kdyby přeci malá
vzpomínka vzešla, pak at' je to na ty veselejší chvíle a případně
na náš „šlojs" v „Landwirčoftu"
Tvá partnerka ze sena léta 1943
Ahoj a zdař Bůh

:: HOLKA-KLUK   RUTH B   2.VII.45

Remember Terezín as little as possible but if a small memory
comes up just the same, then may it be of those happier moments
like our "sluice" at "Landwirtschaft" [farm work]
Your haying partner of summer 1943
Bye-bye and fare well!

:: GIRL-BOY   RUTH B.   07.02.45

In camp jargon, to "sluice" meant to purloin, take, or steal. Ruth Barsiová (b. 17 August 1926) refers here to instances when she and Mariánka "stole" fresh vegetables when they were assigned to farm work in the summer of 1943. Mariánka describes Ruth as a beautiful, tall, and very strong girl, which would have made her a welcome haying partner. Barsiová was deported to Auschwitz on 1 October 1944. She survived and was liberated in Mauthausen.

2.VII.45

Na Terezín co nejméně vzpomínej, ale kdyby přeci malá vzpomínka vzešla, pak ať je to na ty veselejší chvíle a případně na náš "šlojs" v "Landwirtschaftu"

Tvá partnerka ze sena

léta 1943

Ahoj a zdař Bůh

Kotka-Klnk

Ruth B.

46

"Proč bychom se netěšili?" Byla to Rafíčkova hudba
a lidskost, která nám pomáhala v Terezíně z toho nejhoršího, vid'?
V upomínku na jeho vděčnou obdivovatelku
:: TRUDA BONDYOVÁ UŽ V PRAZA V KVĚTNU 1946

"Why not rejoice?" It was Rafíček's music and humanity that
helped us in Terezín during the worst of times, right?
In memory of his grateful admirer
:: TRUDA BONDYOVÁ ALREADY IN PRAGUE IN MAY 1946

Truda (Gertruda; also Trudy) Bondyová, born 15 April 1922, and her older sister Alice, born 26 February 1921 (see next entry), were deported from Prague to Terezín on 30 January 1942. Of the 1,000 Jews on that transport, 906 died or were killed; 94 lived to be liberated. These sisters were among the survivors. They sang with Mariánka in the chorus of Schächter's productions. Their words and Trudy's use of an affectionate diminutive of his name show that they, too, treasured their experience with Schächter.

"Proč bychom se netěšili?"
Byla to Rafičkova hudba
a lidkost, která nám pomáhala v Terezíně z toho
nejhoršího, viď?

V upomínku na jeho
vděčnou obdivovatelku
Trudu Bondyovou.
Už v Praze v květnu 1946.

47

—a hned vedle Trudy musí samozřejmě být Alice, která sdílí
její a současně Tvé názory. „Prodanka", „Requiem", „Hubička"—
a ovšem naše „Česká píseň"— tot' byly záblesky světla v
terezínském temnu.

:: ALICE BONDYOVÁ   PRAHA, KVĚTEN 1946

—and right next to Trudy there of course has to be Alice, who
shares her views and also at the same time yours. "The Bartered
Bride," "Requiem," "The Kiss," and of course our "Czech
Song"— those were the flashes of light in the Terezín darkness.

:: ALICE BONDYOVÁ   PRAGUE, MAY 1946

Alice Bondyová was Trudy's sister.

... a hned vedle Trudy
nesmí samozřejmě být
Alice, která sdílí její
a současně Tvé názory.

„Prodaná", „Requiem",
„Hubička" – a ovšem
naše „Česká píseň" –
toť byly záblesky světla
v terezínském šeru.

Alice Boudyová

Praha, Kočen 1946.

48

:: V PRAZE ŠONY SINGER   :: IN PRAGUE ŠONY SINGER

27. IX. 1946   09.27.1946

Born in Romania, Šony (Alexander, sometimes called Shani) Singer moved to Prague before the war, where he worked as a tailor. He developed his vocal talent in Terezín, sometimes playing (among others) the part of Vašek in The Bartered Bride. *(Jehuda Jacob Goldring also sang this part; see entry 51.) The music he noted here comprises two excerpts from that opera. Singer returned to Prague after liberation. He joined the chorus of the Grand Opera and had minor solo parts from time to time. One such appearance with the Czech Philharmonic led to a position as cantor in Johannesburg, South Africa.*

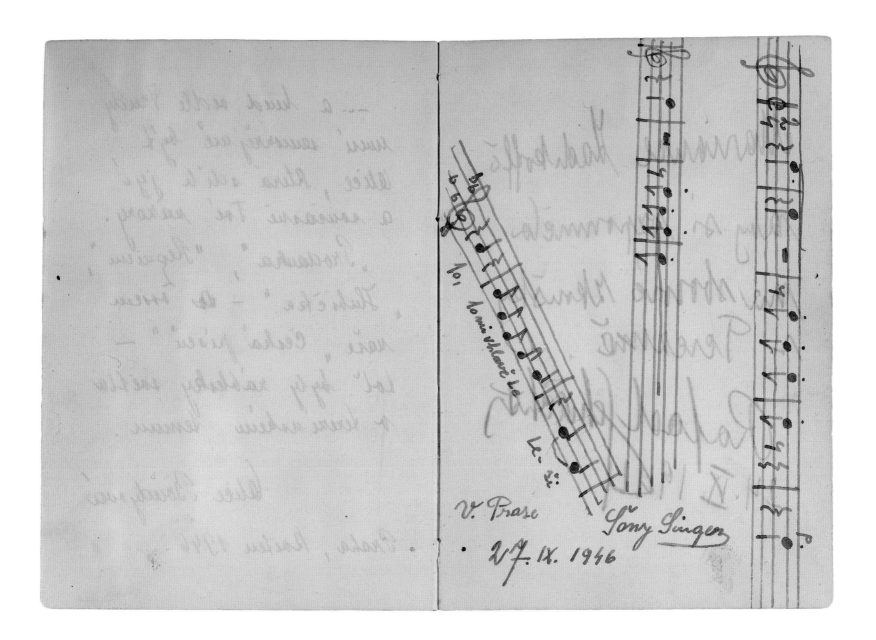

V. Praze
27. IX. 1946

Tony Singer

49

Mariánce Zadikoffé,
aby si vzpomněla na sborové zkoušky v Terezině.

:: RAFAEL SCHÄCHTER   24.IX.1944

For Mariánka Zadikoff
to remember the chorus rehearsals in Terezín.

:: RAFAEL SCHÄCHTER   09.24.1944

In souvenire

:: DAVID GRÜNFELD   TEREZÍN 22.IX.44

As a memento

:: DAVID GRÜNFELD   TEREZÍN 09.22.44

A towering figure in the musical life of Terezín and the personal lives of those who sang with him, Rafael Schächter was born in Braila, Romania, in May 1905 and was killed in Auschwitz in October 1944. Schächter had studied music in Brno and at the Prague Conservatory during the interwar years. A choral conductor and a pianist, Schächter established a group called the Chamber Music Opera and was in great demand as a vocal coach. He brought his passion for music, organizational talent, and expertise with vocal music to his productions in Terezín.

David Grünfeld was very important to Mariánka in Terezín. A gifted tenor who had begun to make his mark in the music world before the war, Grünfeld sang in Schächter's productions, including The Requiem.

Born in Uzhgorod (Ruthenia, then part of Austria-Hungary, later of Czechoslovakia, now of Ukraine) in 1915, Grünfeld studied music in Prague. He continued to develop his talent in Terezín. Deported to Auschwitz in October 1944, he was force-marched back to Terezín more dead than alive the following April. Mariánka happened to be on an agricultural detail at the time, planting spinach. She spotted Grünfeld, emaciated, ill, covered with pus-filled sores, shuffling into the camp with a group of other prisoners from the east. "Absolutely no face; only his beautiful eyes. The eyes were the same, but it was the face of a dead man. I put his arm around my shoulder and I held him around the waist . . . I went begging from door to door to door to door [from people] who had saved for the last days something from home that was three or four years old by now. A tiny little cloth bag of rice; a tiny little cloth bag with oatmeal. God knows how full of dust or dirt it was. But they gave it to me. I was able to go to feed him every single morning before I went to work [and] this tremendously big wish of mine [to see him alive] was fulfilled." Their friendship continued when both returned to Prague after liberation.

Grünfeld immigrated to the United States, where he sang under the name David Garen. He enjoyed an active and successful career as a member of the National Broadcasting Company Opera, a recording artist, and a soloist with a number of major symphonies. He became a cantor for the Huntington Jewish Center in New York (1961), a position he held for two years until his death in 1963.

The music is an excerpt from Bizet's Carmen.

Mariance Zadikoffő

aby si vzpomněla

na sborové zkoušky

v Terezíně.

Rafael Schächter

24. IX. 1944

In souvenire [signature]

Terezín 22. IX. 44

50

Der kleinen u. unterspieltesten Tochter
eines großen Vaters, von dem sie gar
kein Talent geerbt hat—als unverfälscht
„Sie" zu sein. Bleibe weiter künstlerisch
unbelastet— aber so wie Du bist. Zur
Erinnerung an Deine „Rechtsanwaltszeit"
und Deinen :: HANS HOFER   KOMIKER a.D.
PRAG 14.XI.45

For the small and most underplayed
daughter of a great father, from whom she
has not inherited any talent—but the one
to be purely "herself." Remain artistically
unburdened—but exactly the way you are.
In memory of your "legal times" and of

:: HANS HOFER   RETIRED COMEDIAN   PRAGUE 11.14.45

To Marianne and Eric

Two days on the farm means much more than two weeks in New
York with all the Rembrandts and other great painters.

We both love the peace and the nice friends on it.

:: WILLIAM & OLGA HINTZMAN   MAY 3/60

*The cabaret performer, actor, and director Hans Hofer was an active participant in the musical
life of Terezín. Known best for his revues, which had sketches, songs, and witty scenes, Hofer also
served as assistant to Kurt Gerron, the director of the Nazi propaganda film* Theresienstadt: A
Documentary from the Jewish Settlement Area.

*Artists William and Olga Hintzman were friends of the Zadikow family before and during the
war. They immigrated to Canada after the war, and they visited Mariánka, her husband Eric
May, and her mother Hilda when the Mays owned a chicken farm.*

der kleinen g unterspielten
Tochter eines großen Vaters,
von dem sie gar kein Talent
geerbt hat – als unverfälscht
„Sie" zu sein. Bleibe weiter
künstlerisch unbelastet –
aber so wie Du bist.

Zur Erinnerung
an Deine „Rechtsanwaltszeit"
und seinen
Prag 14. XI 25   [signature]
Kommissar a. D.

To Marianne and
Eric
Two days on the farm
means much more
than two weeks in
new york with all the
Rembrandts and other
great painters
we both love the
peace and the niece
friend or it
[signatures] William   Olga
Je.
may 3/50.

5I

Ruhe ist eine gute und angenehme Sache.

:: DORA GOLDRING

Rest is a good and pleasant thing.

:: DORA GOLDRING

זכר לצ{יאת טרזין

:: לחברתי מרימבאהבה
יהודהיצקב גולדרינג
טרזין צרב יום כפור
תש״ה

This is in memory of leaving Terezín

:: WITH LOVE TO MY FRIEND, MIRIAM
JEHUDA JACOB GOLDRING
TEREZÍN, EVE OF YOM KIPPUR
1944

Dora Goldring was married to Jehuda Jacob (also spelled Jakob) Goldring. Born 13 February 1915, Dora was deported to Terezín from Prague on 2 July 1942 with her husband. The couple was shipped to Auschwitz on 16 October 1944. Dora Goldring did not survive.

Cantor Jehuda Jacob Goldring (often called Yankl) participated in the secular and religious musical life of Terezín. He sang in the first full vocal concert in the courtyard of the Hamburg barracks in June 1942, officiated as cantor at the central ceremony in honor of the inmates' first Rosh Hashanah in Terezín, and played the part of Vašek in the premiere performance of The Bartered Bride *two months later, in November. However, he refused, on religious grounds, to sing the Verdi Requiem. He would not participate in the production of a mass for the dead. Goldring nevertheless continued to be active, making his debut as an oratorio singer in Haydn's* The Creation *in February 1944. Deported with his wife to Auschwitz in October, Yankl survived and was liberated in Friedland, a subcamp of Gross-Rosen. He immigrated to the United States after the war. Mariánka and he visited twice and they corresponded until his death.*

Ruhe ist eine
gute und angenehme
Sache.

Dora Zebbing

דבר אליה טרבן

בסיב בר

חברתו מרים

ו]זוכרה ותקף

לגבירתי

גרין אוגוסט

תרס"ז

52

Meiner lieben Marianne
zur Erinnerung an eine zwar kurze, aber sehr schöne Zeit in
Theresienstadt. :: DEINE WERA SCHWEITZER   14 JUNI 1945

To my dear Marianne
As a remembrance of the a very short but also very beautiful
time in Theresienstadt. :: YOUR WERA SCHWEITZER   14 JUNE 1945

Wera Schweitzer stayed with Mariánka in Terezín after liberation.

Meiner lieben Marianne
zur Erinnerung
an eine zwar kurze, aber sehr
schöne Zeit in
Theresienstadt.
Deine
Wera Schweitzer

14. Juni 1945

53

Da die Feuerwehr in Theresienstadt nie fehlen dürfte, soll sie auch in diesem Erinnerungsbuch aufscheinen! Erinnern Sie sich oft an die Abt. Feuerwehr und Luftschutz und an deren Kommandanten. :: ING. LEO HOLZER   THERESIENSTADT, 15.VI.1945

Since the fire department in Theresienstadt was always on call, it should also appear in this memory book. Remember often the Dep't. of Fire and Air-Raid and its chief.

:: ENGINEER LEO HOLZER   THERESIENSTADT, 06.15.1945

Leo Holzer ran the fifty-man fire brigade in Terezín, which extinguished some 800 fires at the camp. The men and their chief lived in L502. In the fall of 1944, all fifty firemen were sent to Auschwitz. Only Holzer remained in Terezín, and he survived. Mariánka remembers him as "extremely capable" and a "good person."

Da die Feuerwehr in Theresienstadt
nie fehlen durfte, soll sie auch
in diesem Erinnerungsbuche
aufscheinen! Erinnern Sie sich
öfters an die Abt. Feuerwehr
und Luftschutz und an
deren Kommandanten

Theresienstadt, 15. VI. 1945

54

Mariánce
Miluj všechny, věř málokterým neurážej nikoho, at' se Ti
vysmívají pro Tvé mlčení, jen ne když pro Tvou řeč!
:: JÁJA   TEREZÍN 5./XI.44

To Mariánka
Love all, trust few, offend no one, let them laugh at you for your
silence but not for your words! :: JÁJA   TEREZÍN 11.5.1944

*Jája (Jarmila) Adlerová (Adler-Schick), born 23 March 1927, was deported to Terezín from
Prague on 4 September 1942. A member of Schächter's chorus, she sang in the alto group.
Adlerová remained in Terezín, survived, and ultimately immigrated to Austria. Mariánka saw
her in Prague after the war and once, in 1993, in the United States.*

Terezín 5./XI. 44.

Miluj všechny,
věř málokterým
neuražej nikoho,
ať se Ti vysmívají pro
Tvé mlčení,
jen ne když pro Tvou řeč!

Mariánce

Jája.

55

Marianne!
Muse der Freizeit, geniess Deine Freizeit,
in der so sehnlichst erwarteten,
endlich angebrochenen
Zeit der Freiheit!
:: DEINE LILY OLDEN IM BEFREITEN THERESIENSTADT, 16.V.45.

Marianne!
You muse of free time, enjoy your free time, in the eagerly
longed for and finally beginning time of freedom!
:: YOUR LILY OLDEN IN LIBERATED THERESIENSTADT, 05.16.45

In this entry, Lily Olden plays on the word "Freizeit" to refer to the camp-regulated "free time"
and their new "free time" with liberation. No information about Lily Olden is available.

Marianne!

Nun der Freizeit, genieß Deine Freizeit, in der so schmerzlich erwarteten, endlich angebrochenen Zeit

der Freiheit!

Denk' Deiner Mutter

Im besetzten Theresienstadt,
16. 3. 45

56

Feiger Gedanken
Bängliches Schwanken
Wendet kein Unheil—
Macht Dich nicht frei!

Allen Gewalten
Zum Trutz sich erhalten,
Nimmer sich beugen,
Kräftig sich zeigen
Rufet die Arme der
Götter herbei!
In herzlichem Gedanken

:: DORA CZAPSKI
THERESIENSTADT, D. 2.7.1945

Cowardly thoughts
Wavering fears
do not reverse misfortune
do not set you free.

Defying all powers
preserving ourselves
never humbly groveling
showing our strength
will summon the
embrace of the gods!
In heartfelt thoughts

:: DORA CZAPSKI
THERESIENSTADT, 07.02.1945

Dora Czapski served as Leo Baeck's (entry 92) housekeeper in Terezín. In addition to cleaning his living quarters, she looked after the rabbi solicitously. According to Mariánka, this protected her from deportation. The text she inscribed here is by Goethe. Brahms set it to music (op. 93a, 5, and op. 95). Later, Ernest Vietor did the same (op. 10). Quoted from memory, the first stanza is incomplete. The full version reads:

Feiger Gedanken
Bängliches Schwanken,
Weibisches Zagen,
Ängstliches Klagen
Wendet kein Elend,
Macht Dich nicht frei.

Allen Gewalten
Zum Trutz sich erhalten,
Nimmer sich beugen,
Kräftig sich zeigen
Rufet die Arme der
Götter herbei!

There are a few standard translations. The following is by Emily Ezust:

Cowardly thoughts,
timid shaking,
womanish hesitation,
fearful lamentation—
they ward off no misery,
they do not make you free.

Gathering all your forces
for the offensive
never to give way,
showing yourself powerful:
this calls the arms
of the Gods to your side!

Feiger Gedanken
Bängliches Schwanken
Wendet kein Unheil –
Macht Dich nicht frei!
Allen Gewalten
Zum Trutz sich erhalten,
Nimmer sich beugen,
Kräftig sich zeigen
Rufet die Arme der
Götter herbei!

In herzlichem Gedanken
Dora Czapski.

Theresienstadt, d. 2. 7. 1945.

57

Za každou krůpěj radosti zaplatíš pohár žalu!

:: M. SEDLAŘÍKOVÁ   3.4.1946

For each drop of joy you pay with a chalice of sorrow!

:: M. SEDLAŘÍKOVÁ   04.03.1946

Markéta Sedlaříková (b. 1 October 1906) was deported to Terezín on 31 January 1945 in a forced-labor detail composed primarily of people who previously had been protected for one reason or another. After the war, she worked with Mariánka at the Jewish Community Center in Prague.

Za každou krůpěj
radosti zaplatíš
pohár žalu!

M. Sedlaříková

3./4. 1946

58

Te decet hymnus!   To you a hymn is due!

:: HANKA4.X.1944   :: HANKA10.04.1944

Hanka Angerová sang with Mariánka in Schächter's production of Verdi's Requiem. *The text is from* The Requiem; *the image is Hanka herself from the back. Hanka survived, returned to Prague, and became a successful painter after the war. Mariánka saw her again half a century later, in 1995.*

Te decet hymnus!

Hanka.   4. X. 1944.

59

Na památku na pytlíčky.
Tvoje přítelkyně :: ZDĚNKA TEREZÍN 19/IV.1945

To remember the pouches.
Your friend, :: ZDĚNKA TEREZÍN 04.19.1945

Zdenka worked with Mariánka in the Galanteriewarenerzeugung (notions workshop), where they made thousands of tobacco pouches for the German army.

Na památku na pytlíčky

Tvoje přítelkyně

Zdeňka

60

Zur ewigen Erinnerung an Deinen Mitarbeiter vom Pferdestall.

:: OTTO HOCHNER MIT DER DICKEN UNTERLIPPE. TEREZÍN 27.6.45

As a lasting memory from your co-worker from the horse stables.

:: OTTO HOCHNER THE ONE WITH THE FAT LOWER LIP. TEREZÍN 06.27.45

Otto Hochner worked with Mariánka in the agricultural detail in Terezín toward the end of the war.

Zur ewigen Erinnerung
an Deinen Mitarbeiter
vom Pferdestall.

Otto Hahn

mit der dicken Unterlippe.

Terezin 24.6.45

6I

Marianko!

Jistě budeš dlouko vzpomínat na ony chvíle, kdy celá smutná jsi přišla do „právního" si stěžovat na Tvoje potravinové lístky s „hnusným" označením.

Teď je to ale za Tebou, máš správné lístky, pracuješ, budeš mít i přídavkové. Musím říci, že je to v dnešní době to nejlepší.

Mimo to Ti ale ještě přeji do budoucna vše další nejlepší.
:: MARTA PEROUTKOVÁ-SACHSELOVÁ   17.9.1945

Mariánka!

It will probably be for some time that you will remember how you came sad to the "legal department" complaining about your ration tickets with the "disgusting" stamp.

But that all is behind you now, you have the correct ration tickets, you are working, and you will receive some additional tickets. I must say that these days that is the best one can get.

But besides all this, I also wish you everything best for the future.
:: MARTA PEROUTKOVÁ-SACHSELOVÁ.   09.17.1945

The stamps on Mariánka's and Hilda's papers both during and after the war marked them as despised members of society. In occupied Prague, their ration cards carried the J stamp for Jude *(Jew). In postwar Prague, they were marked with a D for* Deutsche *(German, which at the time meant Nazi). Marta Peroutková-Sachselová and Mariánka worked together in the legal department of the Jewish Community Center for two years.*

Mariańko !

Jistě budeš dlouho vzpomínat na ony chvíle, kdy celá smutná jsi přišla do „právního" si stěžovat na Tvoje potravinové lístky s „hnusným" označením.

Teď je to ale za Tebou, máš správné lístky, pracuješ, budeš mít i přídavkové. Musím říci, že je to v dnešní době to nejlepší.

Mimo to Ti ale ještě přeji do budoucna vše další nejlepší.

Marta Peroutková–Sachselová

17./9. 1945.

62

A co nedá člověk za svobodu?
F. M. Dostojevskij

Který milionář, když by mu zadrhli krk petlici, nedal by
všechny své miliony za jediný doušek vzduchu?
V upomínku :: HANUŠ KOLDAVSKÝ V PRAZE, DNE 12.IX.45.

What would man not give for freedom?
F. M. Dostoyevsky

Which millionaire, when the noose would tighten around his
throat, would not give all his millions for a single breath of air?
In memory :: HANUŠ KOLDAVSKÝ IN PRAGUE, 09.12.45

Hanuš Koldavský worked at the Jewish Community Center of Prague.

F. M. Dostojevskij.

co nedá člověk za
svobodu?

Který milionář, když by mu
zadrhli krk petlicí,
nedal by všechny své miliony
za jediný doušek vzduchu?

Supomínku

Henud Koldovský

V Praze, dne 12. XI. 45.

6₃

Milá Marjánko,

nezapomeň na Haničku a vůbec to je blbý, když
člověk na sebe ~~na~~ tak myslí, ale já to myslím vážně.

Věřím, že se ještě v životě potkáme—a to už
nebude srab!!!

:: TVÁ HANKA   POSLEDNÍ VEČER V TEREZÍNĚ 21./X. 44
Č. TR. 1332

Dear Mariánka,

Do not forget Hanička and I know it is kind of dumb
when people think of themselves but I mean it for real.

I believe that we shall meet again in this life—and
than that life won't be crap anymore!!!

:: YOUR HANKA   LAST EVENING IN TEREZÍN 10.21.44
TR[ANSPORT] N[UMBER] 1332

Transports left Terezín two or three days after inmates received their deportation notices. No one knew precisely when the trains would roll. For the designated victims, such as Hanka, each day might be the last in the camp. Her transport of 1,715 people left Terezín for Auschwitz on 23 October 1944. The teenaged Hanka, a Schächter chorister, was not among the 159 who survived.

CO znedá člověk za

Milá Marjánko,

nezapomeň na Hanečku
vůbec to já blbý, kdyžtě
člověk na sebe sám tak
myslí, ale já to myslím
vážně.

Věřím, že se jistě v životě
potkáme — a to se nebude
probůh!!! Tvá Hanka

Poslední večer v tvrdčírně 21/8. 44
i tr. 1532

64

:: [IN MIRROR WRITING] ZUR EWIGEN ERINNERUNG
VON VATER KANTOR   26.IV.1958

:: [IN MIRROR WRITING] FOR LASTING MEMORY
FROM FATHER KANTOR   04.26.1958

The artist Alfred Kantor (b. 7 November 1923 in Prague) was deported to Terezín with transport "J" from Prague on 4 December 1941. Kantor drew hundreds of sketches and pictures depicting daily life in Terezín, Auschwitz, and Schwarzheide. He destroyed most of his drawings at the time for fear they would be discovered and he would be killed. A few were smuggled out of the camps. Kantor recreated his work from memory immediately after liberation, and published 127 images in The Book of Alfred Kantor *(New York: McGraw-Hill, 1971). This collection remains an important visual record of Nazi atrocities and a poignant memorial to its victims. Kantor's reflections upon the significance of art for him as an inmate mirror Mariánka's assessment of the role of music for her. "My commitment to drawing came out of a deep instinct of self-preservation and undoubtedly helped me to deny the unimaginable horrors of that time," Kantor explained twenty-five years later. "By taking the role of 'observer' I could at least for a few moments detach myself from what was going on in Auschwitz and was therefore better able to hold together the threads of sanity."Art did not keep him alive— he had luck and food packages from a sister in Prague (who was married to a non-Jew and thus managed to elude deportation) to thank for that—but it kept him whole. Deported to Auschwitz on 15 December 1943, Kantor was sent in June 1944 to Schwarzheide (near Dresden), where he and other slave laborers worked twelve-hour shifts rebuilding a synthetic fuel plant. He was one of only 175 prisoners out of 1,000 to survive a death march back to Terezín. He immigrated to the United States after the war and died in Yarmouth, Maine, on 16 January 2003.*

65

Ein paar Worte zum Gedenken, / Wünscht Marianne sich. / Will mich drum nicht lang bedenken, / Weißt es ja: gern hab ich Dich.

Gern hör' ich Dein frohes Singen, / Deines Sprechens heitern Klang, / Deines Lachens lautes Klingen, / Sehe gern die Pfirsichwang.

Seh gern leuchten Deine Augen, / Wenn Begeisterung Dich hebt, / Denn es will zu dem nur taugen, / Der hoch über'm Alltag schwebt.

Selbstlos schenkst Du her Dein Essen, / Stets würd mir's Errin'rung sein. / Wirst auch Du mich nicht vergessen? / Ich, gewiss, gedenke Dein! :: ALICE MOSER   25 OKTOBER 1944

Marianne wishes for a few words / For memory's sake. / I will not think about it long / Because you know I like you.

I am glad to hear your joyful singing, / Your cheerful way of speaking, / Your bright laughter. / I am glad to see your peachy cheeks.

I gladly see the light in your eyes / When you are uplifted by enthusiasm. / This trait belongs only to those / Who float high above the everyday drudgery.

Unselfishly you give your food to someone else. / How could I ever forget you? / Will you remember me too? / I certainly won't forget you! :: ALICE MOSER   25 OCTOBER 1944

Alice Moser worked in the Galanteriewarenerzeugung *(notions workshop) with Mariánka for two years or more. They were very fond of each other.*

Ein paar Worte zum Gedenken,
Wünschet Marianne sich.
Will mich drum nicht lang bedenken,
Weiß es ja: gern hab ich Dich.

Gern hör' ich Dein frohes Singen,
Deines Sprechens heitern Klang,
Deines Lachens lautes Klingen,
Sehe gern die Pfirsichwang.

Seh gern leuchten deine Augen,
Wenn Begeisterung Dich belebt,
Denn es will zu Dem nur taugen,
Der hoch überm Alltag schwebt.

Selbstlos schenkst Du her Dein Essen,
Stets wird mir's Erinn'rung sein.
Wirst auch Du mich nicht vergessen?
Ich, gewiss, gedenke Dein!

Alice Moser.

25. Oktober 1944.

66

Professor Hermann Hessel Leydensdorff (b. 1891), an academic and a violinist, was deported from the Netherlands to Terezín in 1944. Thus he entered the cultural life of the camp when many Czech and German musicians were sent to Auschwitz. Well respected in the music world before the war, Leydensdorff proved an active participant in Terezín productions. He played with pianists Alice Sommer Herz (entry 84) and Elsa Schiller, and he took over the concertmaster's chair in orchestras led by Peter Deutsch, who favored light music, and Leo Pappenheim (entry 93), who conducted opera scores. Leydensdorff survived the war and returned to the Netherlands, where he lived in the town of Naarden until his death.

H. Leykauff

67

:: 3.VII.1945
TERASA V TEREZÍNĚ

:: 07.03.1945
TERRACE IN TEREZÍN

Mariánka and Hilda moved into the room of another inmate, K. Burešová, when Burešová left Terezín for Prague after liberation in May 1945. Hilda sketched that room, with its wooden balcony, a few months later.

3. VII. 1945.

Белаз в Березин

68

Wir wollen nicht wägen wie es zwischen Händlern üblig ist—Gut um Gut, Ware um Ware, sondern wir wollen geben und schenken, uns beschenken und dankbar sein.

In Liebe

:: DEINE GILDA (ROSENTHAL) [*added in different handwriting*]
2.10.44 THERESIENSTADT

We do not want to weigh as traders do—goods for goods, wares for wares, but rather we want to give and give presents, receive presents, and be grateful.

In love

:: YOUR GILDA
THERESIENSTADT 10.2.44

Teaching was an accepted and common way for inmates to earn extra food or goods from one another. Nevertheless, Gilda Rosenthal did not charge Mariánka for the Hebrew lessons she gave her in Terezín.

Wir wollen nicht wägen,
wie es zwischen Händlern
üblich ist - Gut um Gut,
Ware um Ware, sondern
wir wollen geben und
schenken, und beschenken
lassen und dankbar
sein.

In Liebe
Deine Hilde (Rosenthal?)

2.10. 44. Theresien-
stadt

69

Unserer Spedition zur
Erinnerung an manche
„Schwere" Stunde.

:: MARION PODOLIER
HILDE ARONSON-LINDT
HEDDA GRAB-KERNMAYR
25.III.45

To our luggage carrier in order
to remember many a "heavy"
hour.

:: MARION PODOLIER
HILDE ARONSON-LINDT
HEDDA GRAB-KERNMAYR
03.25.45

Marion Podolier (soprano) and Hilda Aronson-Lindt (mezzo-soprano) were two of the four soloists in Schächter's production of Verdi's Requiem. *Hedda (Hedvika) Grab-Kermayr, also known as Hedda Grabová, served as a "talent scout" for Schächter: she brought Mariánka into that circle. Grab-Kernmayer performed in many operas and provided much energy for other musical efforts. She was a central force behind the*

Freizeitgestaltung *(leisure time activities)—indeed, Mariánka called her "the mother of* Freizeitgestaltung, *although her name is not listed among the officials of that department. Podolier and Aronson-Lindt performed in numerous operas and* Liederabende *(song evenings). All three women remained in Terezín until liberation. Grabová immigrated to Israel and then to Denver, Colorado, where she established a small musical ensemble.*

Mariánka kept in touch with Grabová until the older woman's death.

The entry refers both to Mariánka's help moving their mattresses and luggage (because the young men had been deported) and to her support through emotionally and psychologically heavy times.

Unserer Spedition
zur Erinnerung an
manche „schwere" Stunde.

Marion Portier
Hilde Aronson-Lind
Hedda Grab-Kernmayr

25. III. 45.

70

Ter herinnering aan de verheffende Muziek uitvoeringen bij de „Freizeit" gedurende onze ballingschap in Terezin.

:: J. POPPELSDORF   EERST VIOLIST VAN HET „CONCERTGEBOUW-ORKEST"

TEREZÍN 30 MEI 1945

In memory of the uplifting "Freizeit" music performances during our exile in Terezín.

:: J[UDA] POPPELSDORF   FIRST VIOLIST OF THE CONCERTGEBOUW ORCHESTRA

TEREZÍN 30 MAY 1945

Juda Poppelsdorf was a violist in the Concertgebouw Orchestra of Amsterdam from 1898 to 1940, earning the chair of first violist.

Ter herinnering aan de
beheffende Muziek uitvoering
bij de "Freizeit" gedurende
onze ballingschap in
Terezin.

[handtekening]

1e Violist van het
"Concertgebouw-Orkest"
Amsterdam.

Terezin 30 Mei 1945.

7I

Meiner lieben Nichte Marianne alles, alles Gute fürs Leben.

:: TANTE TONI   TEREZÍN 1945 MAI–JUNI

To my dear niece Marianne, all the very best for her life.

:: AUNT TONI   TEREZÍN 1945 MAY–JUNE

Wie oft Sie auch immer dieses Büchlein zur Hand nehmen
werden, dann verweilen Sie bitte auch auf dieser Seite einen
kleinen Augenblick und versuchen Sie den folgenden Namen mit
einem freundlichen Lächeln auszusprechen!

:: HANS GRÜNWALD   THERESIENSTADT, 1945

No matter how often you hold this little book in your hand,
please stay on this page for a little while and try to pronounce
the following name with a friendly smile!

:: HANS GRÜNWALD   THERESIENSTADT, 1945

Toni Zadikow was Mariánka's aunt; her husband was Mariánka's father's brother. Paul Zadikow was deported to Auschwitz, where he was killed. His widow survived.

Hans Grünwald sang in Terezín with a group that performed scenes from The Tales of Hoffmann.

Meiner lieben Nichte
Mariane alles, alles Gute
für's Leben.
               Tante Toni

Terezín 1945 - Mai-Juni

Wie oft Sie auch immer
dieses Büchlein zur Hand
nehmen werden, dann
verweilen Sie bitte auch auf dieser
Seite einen kleinen Augenblick
und versuchen Sie den folgenden
Namen mit einem freundlichen
Lächeln auszusprechen!

               Hans Grünwald

Theresienstadt, 1945.

72

Писать ж вольно я ришился / любов заставила миня / На сердце грустно / Поэтому и пишу Я. / Миша.

Посседний нынишний динечек / гуляю с вами я друзя. / А завтра рано Чуть свиточек / уижаю Я. / Миша.

Пишу с далёкого края / где вечно царить тишена / где люди живут в наслаждени / но только не Я. / Миша.

Лови минуты счастя они / бывають времем хороши / но не узнавши человека / не откривай своей души.
:: Миша   27.6.45

I have decided to write freely. / Love forced me to. / My heart is heavy, / That's why I, Misha, am writing.

This is the very last day / That I celebrate with you, my friends. / And tomorrow early at dawn, / I, Misha, am leaving.

I am writing from a faraway land / Where eternal silence reigns, / Where people live in joy, / Except for me, Misha.

Seize the moments of happiness. / Now and then they are good. But if you do not know the person, / Do not open your soul.
:: MISHA   6.27.45

This entry by a Soviet soldier, Misha, was written at his insistence, not Mariánka's request. Misha wanted to marry Mariánka and take her back to the Ukraine with him. At the time and in retrospect she was relieved that his intentions were honorable; rape was common. She refused Misha's offer by pretending that another inmate, Peter Langweil, was her fiancé.

Писать не вольно
27/6-45г. Я Решился Любов
заставила меня
На сердце грустно
Потому и пишу Я!..
    Миша.

Последний нынешний
Денёчек гуляю с вами
Я друзья А завтра рано
чуть светочек уйдем
Я, Миша.

Пишу с далёкого края
где венно царит тишена
где люди живут в лесла-
недели но только и Я-Миша.

Лови Минуты
счастя они бывают
времем хороши
но не узнавши
человека не открывай
своей души.
    Миша.

73

Podaná ruka mimojdoucímu, který se ohlížel po ní, / jest u cesty smutné u cesty dlouhé / květ, který voní.

Podaná ruka, zcela prosté gesto / jež čekáním vděčnosti nemaří času, / je ptačí píseň v náhlé samotě / kdy zastesklo se po živém hlasu.

Podaná ruka, větévka tenká / kterou jsi nabídl tonoucí včele, / pomáhá kovat železný řetěz / v němž živé živému věrno / je celé.

Podaná ruka kterékoliv věci / k suětlu deroucí se vedle tebe / svěžejším činí stromů stín / teplejším hvězdnaté nebe.

Vesmírná útěcha line se z věnce / jež tvoříš-přišel-lis pomoci moha. / Podaná ruka na kterémkoliv místě / pravého tvoří Boha.
(Stanislav K. Neumann)

:: EVA   PRAHA V KVĚTNU 1947

An outstretched hand to a passerby / who turned and looked at it / is a fragrant blossom / by a sad path, a long path.

An outstretched hand, this very simple gesture / that does not waste time with expectations of gratitude / is like a bird's song in sudden loneliness / when one longs to hear the voice of another.

An outstretched hand, the thin branch / you offered to a drowning bee, / helps to forge an iron chain / in which all living faithful to the living are.

An outstretched hand to anything / that next to you struggles toward the light / will make the tree shadows fresher / and the starry skies warmer.

Great solace emanates from the wreath / which you create—if you come able to help. / An outstretched hand at whatever place / creates the true God.
(Stanislav K. Neumann)

:: EVA   PRAGUE, MAY 1947

Eva Weissová was deported to Terezín from Brno on 28 January 1942 and sent to Auschwitz eighteen months later, on 18 December 1943. She ultimately was liberated in Christianstadt and returned to Prague after the war. She worked with Mariánka at the Jewish Community Center. Weissová emigrated to England, where, as of 2000, she was still living.

Podaná ruka mimojdoucímu,
který se oblížel po ní,
jest u cesty smutné u cesty dlouhé
květ, který voní.

Podaná ruka, zcela prosté gesto
jež čekáním odvěkosti nemeří čas,
je ptačí píseň v náhlé samotě
kdy zastesklo se po zjevu blesu.

Podaná ruka, větévka tenká
kterou jsi nabídl tonoucí včele,
pomáhá kosod železný řeký
v němž zjné životu věrno je celé.

Podaná ruka kterékoliv věci
k světlu denní se vedle tebe
svěžejším činí stromů stín
teplejším hvězdovité nebe.

Vesmírná útěcha line se z věnce
jež tvoříš – přeblio pomoci ruka.
Podaná ruka na kterémkoliv místě
pravdio tvoří Boha.
                (Stanislav K. Neumann).

                                    Eve.

Praha v květnu 1947.

74

Marianko! Budě-li mýti dlouhou chvíli vzpomeň si na Tvou
kolegyně z Hanné. :: R. BROLLOVOU   TEREZÍN, 17/5. 1945

Mariánka! Should you be bored, remember your colleague
from Hanná. :: R. BROLLOVÁ   TEREZÍN, 05.17.1945

*Regina Brollová was from the Hanná region of Moravia. She survived the war and returned
to Czechoslovakia. Mariánka visited her once in 1946, while she was still in Prague. Brollová
visited Mariánka and her family once in the United States in 1958. The design is in Moravian
peasant style.*

Terezín, 17/5.1945

Mariánko! Budeš-li
míti dlouhou chvíli
vzpomeň si na Svou
kolegyni z Hanné

R. Bollovou

75

Ein paar Jahre später: „Wie hat denn nur die Stadt geheißen, wo ich die kleine Zadikow kennen lernte?!" :: EMO GROAG   IV. 1945.

A few years later: "What was the name of the town where I met the little Zadikow girl?" :: EMO GROAG   APRIL 1945

Emo Groag (b. 25 May 1886), his wife Gertruda (b. 1892), their son Vilém (called Willy, b. 7 August 1914), and his wife Maria (b. 1918) were deported to Terezín on transport AAm from Olomouc, Moravia, on 4 July 1942. Emo worked in the Kartonageabteilung (packaging works), which fashioned various types of boxes out of heavy paper wrapping to ship goods to the Reich. In his entry, he pokes fun at their situation.

Emo's son Willy supervised the girls' home at L410. When the war ended, he collected what remained of the children's artwork and poems. Most of the young people themselves had been deported and killed. Emo returned to Prague in the summer of 1945 with two suitcases filled with their work and donated it the Jewish Museum in Prague. This collection found a wide audience through the publication I Never Saw Another Butterfly.

The family survived (including Willy and Maria's daughter Eva, who was born in Terezín) and emigrated to Israel after the war.

Ein paar Jahre später

EnoGrosz
IV. 1945.

„Wie hat denn nur die Stadt geheißen, wo ich die kleine Zadilaw kennen lernte?!"

76

Své milé spolupracovnici v trvalou vzpomínku a s upřímným
přáním slunné a ničím nezkalené budoucnosti věnuji tyto řádky.
:: DR. WEINBERG V PRAZE 28.XII.45

To my dear co-worker as a lasting memory and with a sincere
wish for a sunny future, not clouded by anything, I dedicate
these words. :: DR. WEINBERG IN PRAGUE, 12.28.45

*Dr. Weinberg was one of the two lawyers for whom Mariánka worked at the Jewish Community
Center in Prague from October 1945 to October 1947.*

Své milé spolupracovnici
v trvalou vzpomínku a
s upřímným přáním slunné
a ničím nezkalené budoucnosti
věnuji tyto řádky.

v Praze 28. XI. 45

77

Hilda Zadikow drew this picture of block L211 at Mariánka's request, to record a specific event that stood for so many others. "It was something very important to me, so I showed it to my mother, and she was kind enough to go the next day and make a drawing."

Mariánka had run into a man on the street who was "totally desperate" because he was due to go on a transport, while his wife and son were to remain in Terezín. "This was [October] 1944 and we had, at that time, absolutely no idea that people would not stay together who left together." Thus it was terribly important to leave on the same transport. Mariánka went to see Berta Katz, his wife, in her quarters in block L211. "She was in her bed with her face turned to the wall and in an unending crying spell. And she said,

'This is the end. This is my death.' . . . That's when I went to Leo Baeck." She asked him to try to postpone the deportation of Mr. Katz; the family would go on the next transport. Together. "And that's what happened. When they got the notice for transport, I visited them again. All three of them were on the floor making a bedroll out of a blanket and wrapping things in it that they would have later on. Of course, they were taken away in Auschwitz and never got them again. But at that time, we didn't know that. And they were actually happy: if we have to leave, we are leaving together." Only Mr. Katz survived.

After the war, Mariánka heard from eyewitnesses about Berta Katz's arrival at Auschwitz. When the doors opened, word spread that women with babies would be

killed. One mother "quickly got off the train," leaving her two small children. Berta Katz "picked up the two children, and with two children, one on each arm, she walked like a hero—which she was—to the gas chambers. These children did not go alone. These children were not left to die alone. These children were held until the last moment."

L 211 TEREZIN.

78

Drawing by Hilda Zadikow

TEREZÍN 1944.

79

Bud taková—jak Tvůj otec byl kterého jsem obdivoval!

:: ING. VOGEL   PRAHA, DNE   31.10.1945

Be like your father, whom I admired!

:: ENGINEER VOGEL   PRAGUE, 10.31.1945

Erich Vogel (b. 30 April 1906), an engineer by profession and trumpet player by passion, organized The Jazz Swingers *in Terezín in January 1943. Vogel was deported from Terezín to Auschwitz on 29 September 1944. He survived and returned to Prague.*

BUĎ TAKOVÁ - JAK TVŮJ OTEC BYL
KTERÉHO JSEM OBDIVOVAL !

PRAHA, DNE
31. 10. 1945

FAST SWING TEMPO

GETTO- SWINGERS THEME-SONG

8o

:: ROHN JULIUS
[*illegible*] TEREZÍN   1945

Věčně tu trčet přece jen nebudem. A pak, až jednuo budeš mít
„volný den" podnikni výlet do Radošovic u Prahy, kde v čp. 246
má svůj wigwam. :: FRANTA KUBIE   24/X. 44

After all, we will not be stuck here forever. And then when you
have "a free day," take a trip to Radošovice near Prague, where
in the house number 246 is his wigwam. :: FRANTA KUBIE   10.24.44

*Franta (František) Kubie was a foreman
at the Galanteriewarenerzeugung (notions
workshop)where Mariánka worked for more
than two years. They became good friends.
Kubie uses the word "wigwam" to mean a
weekend cottage.*

*Deported to Terezín from Prague on 4
December 1941, Kubie was one of the 1,210*

*prisoners to leave the camp for Switzerland
on 5 February 1945. Reichsführer-SS Heinrich
Himmler, at the urging of the former president
of Switzerland Jean-Marie Musy, and with
the support of his masseur Felix Kersten, had
agreed to send a few thousand Jewish inmates
from Terezín to that country. He hoped this
initiative would win the Reich favorable
press reports. It did not. Alarmed, Himmler's*

*underlings Ernst Kaltenbrunner (chief of the
Reich Security Main Office) and Heinrich
Müller (chief of the Gestapo) alerted Hitler,
who told Himmler not to send any more Jews
from Terezín to Switzerland.*

Profes. Julius
Gorl. Terezín
1945

Věčně tu hrát přece jen
nebudem. A tak, až jednou
budeš mít "volný den" podnikni
výlet do Radošovic u Prahy,
kde v čp. 246 má svůj
vigvam
Franta Kučera.
24/X. 44

81

Meinem lieben „fanoušek" zur Erinnerung an die Theresienstädter musikalischen Abende! :: ADA SCHWARZ-KLEIN   21/III 1945

To my dear "little fan" as a memory of the Theresienstadt musical evenings. :: ADA SCHWARZ-KLEIN   03.21.1945

Ada Schwarz-Klein, an alto, was a professional opera and lieder singer. A central figure in the musical life of Terezín, she participated in Schächter's productions as well as in many others. Schwarz-Klein, like Marion Podolier, Hedda Grabová, and Hilde Aronson-Lindt (entry 69), remained in Terezín until liberation and survived.

Meinem lieben
"Januschek" zur
"Erinnerung an
die Theresienstädter
musikalischen Abende!

Ada Schnur-Klein

21/III 1945

82

Aby se Vám podařilo svésti v soulad rozum a cit Vám přeje

:: DR. LEO KRAUS   PRAHA 21/I. 1947

May you succeed in bringing into harmony reason and emotion.
A wish from :: DR. LEO KRAUS   PRAGUE, 01.21.1947

*Mariánka worked with Dr. Leo Kraus after the war at the Jewish Community Center in Prague.
A well-respected physician in Prague before the war, Dr. Kraus was deported to Terezín on 13
July 1943 and shipped to Auschwitz on 23 October 1944. Liberated in Dachau, he returned to
Prague and became head of the medical department of the Jewish Community Center.*

Aby se Vám podaři-
lo vésti v soulad
rozum a cit Vám
přeje

Dr Sukman

V Praze 21/i. 1947.

83

„Es kann die Ehre dieser Welt
Dir keine Ehre geben,
Was Dich in Wahrheit stützt u. hält,
Muss in Dir selber leben."

:: ZUR FRDL. ERINNERUNG AN RABBINER DR. NEUHAUS TEREZÍN 2. JUNI 1945

"The honor of this world
has no honor to give you.
What really supports and sustains you
must reside within you."

:: A FRIENDLY MEMENTO OF RABBI DR. NEUHAUS TEREZÍN, 2 JUNE 1945

Terezín's first Council of Elders was composed of Czech Jews. With the arrival of well over one hundred transports from Germany and Austria between July and October 1942, the national composition of the camp population changed and the Council of Elders was reorganized, in part to reflect this shift. By order of the Camp Headquarters (daily order no. 227, dated 3 October 1942), Dr. Leopold Neuhaus was appointed to the Council.

Leopold Neuhaus (1879–1954) served as a rabbi in Frankfurt from 1934 until he was deported to Terezín in August 1942. When appointed to the Council of Elders, he became deputy head of the internal administration department. This division was in charge of many unenviable tasks: the reception of arriving deportees and the preparation of departing transports; cleaning and security; record keeping; legal matters (including the inmates' court); and the postal service, which formed the only link the Germans permitted between the camp and the outside world.

In addition to these onerous official duties, Rabbi Neuhaus lectured on the Midrash and conducted religious services attended mostly by inmates from Frankfurt. Yankl (Jehuda Jacob) Goldring (see entry 51) sometimes served as cantor at these services.

Neuhaus returned to Frankfurt after the war, where he tried to reestablish a Jewish community. The task was too daunting, the losses too great. In 1946 he emigrated to the United States and settled in Detroit.

In his entry, Dr. Neuhaus quotes a poem by Theodor Fontane. He misremembers only one word in the third line. Fontane's text reads: "Was Dich in Wahrheit hebt und hält."

„Es kann die Ehre dieser Welt
Dir keine Ehre geben,
Was Dich in Wahrheit stützt u. hält,
muss in Dir selber leben.“

Zur freundl. Erinnerung
an Rabbiner Dr. Neuhaus
Terezin 2. Juni 1945.

84

Zur Erinnerung an die lichten Momente in der schweren Zeit in
Theresienstadt. :: IN FREUNDSCHAFT, ALICE SOMMER HERZ   20.IV.45

As a memory of the bright moments during the difficult times in
Theresienstadt. :: IN FRIENDSHIP, ALICE SOMMER HERZ   04.20.45

Born in Prague in 1903, Alice Sommer Herz studied piano at the German Music Academy in Prague. She had earned a fine reputation as a soloist before the war and had given well-received concerts at prestigious venues in Czechoslovakia, Germany, and Sweden. Deported to Terezín in July 1943 with her husband and six-year-old son Rafael, Sommer Herz quickly became a central figure in the musical life of the camp. Some claim that she performed in over one hundred concerts. Sommer Herz was initially assigned to work in the mica factory; her life improved with the increased importance of the Freizeitgestaltung. *The camp administration officially recognized concerts as overtime work, and practice time (two hours a day for pianists when Sommer Herz arrived) was considered work time. She had a wide repertoire but perhaps was most admired for her renditions of Chopin and Beethoven.*

Sommer Herz's husband was deported from Terezín and died in Dachau; she was one of the women artists who remained in Terezín until liberation. Sommer Herz and her son then returned to Czechoslovakia, where she resumed her career. Again she was successful, but she no longer wished to remain in her homeland. In 1949, she and Rafael immigrated to the new state of Israel, where she had an extremely active concert career and joined the faculty of the Music Academy in Jerusalem.

She signed her entry Alice Sommer Herz: Herz was her maiden name and Sommer her married name. She was known as both Herz Sommer and Sommer Herz.

Zur Erinnerung an die
lichten Momente in der
schweren Zeit in Theresienstadt

In Freundschaft

Alice Sommer Herz

85

Meiner lieben Mariánka, zur Erinnerung, an gemeinsam verlebte Näh- und Strickstunden.

:: EINGESCHRIEBEN VON DEINER KOLLEGIN, ELSE FRANK   TEREZÍN, 25./10.44.

To my dear Mariánka, to remember our mutual sewing and knitting classes.

:: ENTERED BY YOUR COLLEAGUE, ELSE FRANK   TEREZÍN, 10.25.44

To obtain extra food and goods, Mariánka knitted industriously in Terezín. Some young men in the electrical department fashioned needles for her out of wire, and she unraveled old, torn sweaters or woolen socks and reused the wool. Mariánka remembers Else Frank as a highly cultured woman, older than she, who knitted as well using proper needles. Else and Mariánka worked in the Galanteriewarenerzeugung (notions workshop) and chatted from time to time as they knitted during their lunch break.

Meiner lieben Marianka
zur Erinnerung, an gemeinsam
verlebte Näh- und Strickstunden

eingeschrieben von deiner
Kollegin
Else Frank.

Terezin, 25./10. 44.

86

In Erinnerung an Sie an die Theresienstädter Freizeit von einem
ganz gewöhnlichen Geiger. :: IN FREUNDSCHAFT, PAUL HERZ   20./ IV.45

In memory of you and of the Theresienstadt free times from a
rather ordinary violinist. :: IN FRIENDSHIP, PAUL HERZ   04.20.45

*Paul (also called Pavel) Herz (b. 19 July 1901) was the brother of Alice Sommer Herz (entry
84) and an accomplished violinist. He was deported to Terezín quite late, on 11 February 1945,
presumably because he was in a protected category. After his arrival, brother and sister often
performed duets.*

20./IV. 45

In Erinnerung an Sie
an die Therenstädter
Freizeit von einem ganz
gewöhnlichen Geiger.

In Freundschaft
Paul Herz.

87

Zůstaň vždy dobrým kamarádem—maš-li času vzpominej na

:: BUSTINA V PRAZE DNE 15.II.1946

Always remain a good friend—and if you have time, remember

:: BUSTIN IN PRAGUE, 02.15.1946

Mariánka remembers that this former inmate "was always ready to lend a helping hand in Terezín."

Zůstaň vždy
    dobrým kamarádem -
maš-li času
    vzpomínej na

Bartma

V Praze dne 15. II. 1946

88

Milá Marjánko,
nikdy Ti to nezapomenu jak jsi se o mě starala při mé nemoci.
:: V UPOMÍNKU VEPSALA TVOJE VDĚČNÁ ZUSKA KLEINOVÁ
21.III.1945 TEREZÍN

Dear Marjánka,
I shall never forget how you cared for me during my illness.
:: IN MEMORY WRITTEN BY YOUR GRATEFUL ZUSKA KLEINOVÁ
03.21.1945 TEREZÍN

Born on 12 January 1932 and deported from Prague to Terezín on 8 July 1943, Zuska (Zuzana Anita) Kleinová was not quite thirteen years old when she wrote this entry. When she fell ill, Mariánka, who was working in the fields at that point, visited her. To give the sick girl a vitamin boost, Mariánka stuffed some edible green leaves into her bra and smuggled them in to her. Kleinová survived and was liberated in Terezín.

Milá Marjánko,

nikdy Ti to nezapomenu
jak jsi se o mě starala
při mé nemoci.

V upomínku

vepsala

Tvoje vděčná

Zuska
Kleinová

21.III.1945 Terezín

89

Denke oft und gern an die schönen Stunden die wir zusammen
auf Heu und Grünfutter verbracht haben. Die vollen Wagen!
Alles Guta für die Zukunft wünscht.

:: DIR, INGE STRÖHL   TEREZÍN 23.VI.45

Do think often and gladly of the wonderful hours we spent
together at haying and at making green fodder. The full wagons!
All the best for the future for you.

:: YOURS, INGE STRÖHL   TEREZÍN 6.23.45

Inge Ströhl, who was a few years younger than Mariánka, had worked with her in the agricultural detail. Their task had been to cut and gather hay, grass, and other fodder. Ströhl wrote this entry after liberation.

Denke oft und gern
an die schönen Stunden
die wir zusammen auf
Heu und Grünfutter ver-
bracht haben.
Die vollen Wagen!

Alles Gute für die
Zukunft wünscht
Dir
Inge Ströhl

Terezin 23. VI. 45

90

Kære Marianne!

Hun lægger os paa Læben hoert godt og kraftligt Ord
til Elskovs sugte Bønner til Sejrens stolte Kor
er Hjertet trangt af Sorgen og svulmes det af Lyst
hun skænker os Tonen som lelle kan vort Bryst

:: MÆNNI RUBEN   11/4—1945

Dear Marianne!

It [music] places every good and powerful word on our lips
From love's quiet appeals to the proud chorus of victory
Whether the heart is beset by worries or swells with desire
It offers us tunes than can soothe our breast

:: MAENNI RUBEN   4.11.1945

Maenni Ruben, one of the Danish Jews deported to Terezín, was a contemporary of Mariánka's and her admirer.

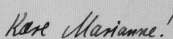

Kære Marianne!

Hun lægger os paa Læben hvert
          godt og kraftigt Ord
til Elskovs sagte Bønner til
          Sejrens stolte Kor
er Hjertet trangt af Sorgen og
          svulmer det af Lyst
hun skænker os Tonen som
          lelle kan vort Bryst

11/4- 1945   Manni Ruben

91

Všechno na tomto světě je omezené,
Jen lidská omezenost je neomezená. Mariance,

:: DAVID   PRAHA, 31.III.1947

Everything in this world has its limits.
Only human ignorance is is infinite. To Mariánka,

:: DAVID   PRAGUE, 03.31.1947

*David was one of a small group of young survivors in their twenties who, as Mariánka explained,
"met frequently in order to help each other live in this 'liberated' but often puzzling world that
had changed so much while we had been in captivity." Most of the young people had been able
to reenter the educational system, either at a university or another kind of school. Mariánka,
deemed by the Czech government to be German, was not eligible for any assistance or support
in this regard, nor did the American Jewish community offer any help when she emigrated to the
United States. She regretted her inability to pursue an education all her life.*

Všechno na tomto světě je
omezené,
Jen lidská omezenost je
neomezená!

Mariance

David.

Praha, 31. III. 1947.

92

In Menschen kämpfen bisweilen die Jahrtausende, aus denen er geworden, mit den Jahren, in denen er ist. Nicht diese, die Jahre, noch vor allem jene, die Jahrtausende, dürfen verdrängt sein, Sie in einander zu entdecken, das ist die Selbstentdeckung des Menschen. Der jüdische Mensch entdeckt sich so.

:: LEO BAECK   THERESIENSTADT, 25 JUNI 1945

Within human hearts the millennia from which man has arisen struggle with those in which he lives. Neither these, the years, much less those, the millennia, should ever be thrust aside. To discover each within the other is the self-discovery of man. The Jew discovers himself in this manner.

:: LEO BAECK   THERESIENSTADT, 25 JUNE 1945

Leo Baeck (1873–1956) was an outstanding German Jewish scholar of the twentieth century and a leader of Progressive Judaism. Educated in rabbinic studies (Conservative and Reform movement training) and in philosophy, Baeck became the rabbi of Berlin's Fasanenstrasse Synagogue, the central synagogue of Reform Judaism, and was appointed professor at the Hochschule für die Wissenschaft des Judentums (Academy for the Study of Judaism). Baeck wrote his most important work, Wesen des Judentums (Essence of Judaism), published in 1905, during this period. According to Baeck, Jewish ethics were the highest expression of an ethical worldview that applied to all people and aimed at the realization of humanity as a whole. The book appeared in many editions and languages. Considered a classic, it is still studied and taught.

By 1914 Baeck was recognized as the most important representative of Reform Judaism. The Great War interrupted his scholarly career; he joined the army as a chaplain and ministered to German Jewish soldiers. An ardent supporter of the Weimar Republic, Baeck served as an expert for Jewish affairs in the Prussian Ministry of Religion and initiated a Jewish-Christian dialogue. Baeck also was active in the Jewish community, mediating between liberal and conservative Jews, participating in Jewish communal organizations and, while not a Zionist, supporting Jewish settlement in Palestine.

When the Nazis came to power in 1933, Baeck devoted himself to defending the Jewish community as president of the Reichsvertretung der Deutschen Juden, the National Association of German Jews. He worked indefatigably for the emigration of Jews but refused to leave himself, even when his family fled to England in 1938. He believed it his obligation to remain with those who could not leave. He continued to try to protect his coreligionists until he was deported to Terezín in 1943. Initially assigned to physical labor like everyone else, the esteemed and elderly rabbi was excused from these duties. He continued to do his part, tending to the sick, giving sermons, and lecturing. His lectures on philosophy attracted huge crowds; some witnesses claim as many as seven hundred people squeezed in to hear the eminent scholar. By then his understanding of Judaism had grown to incorporate both mystery and the mystical. He became a center of dignity and integrity in Terezín, a man who did not bend; he has been compared to a lighthouse in a stormy ocean. It is thus that Mariánka remembers him.

Baeck survived and joined his family in London after the war. He always had believed in interfaith dialogue, and he restarted Jewish-Christian dialogue in Germany in 1948. But he believed that the history of German Judaism had come to a close.

Baeck has not quoted from his own work here; the entry was created for the occasion by this great scholar.

Im Menschen kämpfen bisweilen die Jahrtausende, aus denen er geworden, mit den Jahren, in denen er ist. Nicht diese, die Jahre, noch vor allem jene, die Jahrtausende, dürfen verdrängt sein. Sie in einander zu entdecken, das ist die Selbstentdeckung des Menschen. Der jüdische Mensch entdeckt sich so.

Theresienstadt, 25. Juni 1945.

Leo Baeck.

93

Zur Erinnerung an die Aufführung: „Szenen aus Hoffmanns Erzählungen" :: LEO PAPPENHEIM THERESIENSTADT, 3.5.45

In memory of the performance: "Scenes from the Tales of Hoffmann" :: LEO PAPPENHEIM THERESIENSTADT, 05.03.45

Orchestra conductor Leo Pappenheim (1896–1982) was born in Amsterdam and educated in Germany, where he worked with a number of orchestras and opera companies. When the Nazis came to power in 1933, Pappenheim returned to the Netherlands. Appointed conductor of the Dutch Operaensemble in Rotterdam, he became the leader of the Arnhem Orchestral Society in 1939. Deported to Terezín, Pappenheim took over the remnants of Karel Ančerl's orchestra, breathing new life into the musical world of the camp. He worked with bass singer and stage director Hanuš Thein to deliver a one-hour version of Jacques Offenbach's The Tales of Hoffmann, as charged by Camp Commander Rahm. Pappenheim's entry refers to this production, which proved to be the last major performance in Terezín.

Leo Pappenheim returned to the Netherlands after the war and took up his post at the Arnhem Orchestral Society, which was renamed the Gelders Orchestra. He enjoyed an active career conducting Dutch and German orchestras for thirty years .

Zur Erinnerung an
die Aufführung!
Szenen aus Hoffmanns
„Erzählungen"
                    Leo Pappenheim
Theresienstadt
                    3. 5. 45,

94

V upomínku na společně strávené chvíle, jak ve škole tak v
Terezíně! :: WITTLEROVÁ EVA   V PRAZE, DNE 28.XI.1945

In memory of times spent together in school as well as in
Terezín! :: EVA WITTLEROVÁ   PRAGUE, 11.28.1945

*Eva Wittlerová, born 11 May 1926, was not quite seventeen when she was deported from Prague
to Terezín on 9 March 1943. She was Mariánka's schoolmate, although they were not in the same
class. They met just once after the war.*

V upomínku

na společně prožité
chvíle, jak se škole
tolik v Terezíně!

Wittlerová Ing.

v Praze, dne 28. XI. 45.

95

Přeji Ti moc štěstí, Mariánko!

:: HANA KELLNEROVÁ   29. DUBNA 1945

I wish you lots of happiness, Mariánka!

:: HANA KELLNEROVÁ   29 APRIL 1945

Hana Knellnerová studied art with Charlotta (Lotka) Burešová (entry 108) in the transit camp.

29. dubna 1945

Přeji Ti moc štěstí,
Mariánko!

Hana Kellnerová

96

V upomínku na „tak zvanou" kancelářskou sílu, která o tolik
raději kreslila. :: LOTKA   TEREZÍN, 6.V.45.

In memory of the "so-called" office girl, who so much
preferred to draw. :: LOTKA   TEREZÍN, 05.06.45

*Lotka (Charlotta) Popperová (b. 26 July 1907) and her husband were deported to Terezín from
Pardubice in December 1942. They were sent on to Auschwitz almost immediately, on 23 January
1943. Both survived. Mariánka continued to visit them in Prague and saw their baby shortly
after birth in 1946.*

V upomínku na
„tak zvanou" kancelářskou
sílu, která o tolik raději
kreslila

Lotka

Terezín 6. V. 45.

97

Carpe diem!

:: TVÁ [YOUR] ELLY SCHIFFOVÁ   02.11.46

Elly Schiffová (b. 27 June 1910) was deported from Terezín to Auschwitz on 4 October 1944 and survived to be liberated there. Mariánka met her again in Prague.

Carpe diem!

Tvá

Elly Schiffová

11/II. 46.

98

Sweet are the uses of adversity,
Which, like the toad, ugly and venomous,
Wears yet a precious jewel in his head;
And this our life, exempt from public haunt,
Finds tongues in trees, books in the running brooks,
Sermons in stones, and good in every thing.
(Shakespeare)

With the wish that adversity never may meet you again,
my dear little friend.

:: YOURS SINCERELY
HILDE STEIN-BODANSKY
TEREZÍN—XI. 1944

Hilde Stein-Bodansky (b. 29 April 1890) had been Hilda Zadikow's classmate years earlier, when both were girls in Prague. Deported to Terezín on 8 September 1942, Stein-Bodansky participated in the cultural life of the camp, presenting lectures on literary topics. Liberated in the transit camp, she returned to Prague after the war and remained in contact with the Zadikows. Mariánka took English lessons from her. The quote is from As You Like It, act 2, scene 1.

Sweet are the uses of adversity,
Which, like the toad, ugly and venomous,
Wears yet a precious jewel in his
                                    head;
And this our life, exempt from public
                                    haunt,
Finds tongues in trees, books in the
                                    running brooks,
Sermons in stones, and good in
                    every thing.

                              (Shakespeare.)

With the wish that adversity never may
meet you again, my dear little
friend,

                    Yours sincerely
                    Hilde Stein-Bodansky.

Teverín - XI. 1944

99

Quand on n'a pas ce qu'on aime, on aime ce qu'on a.

:: MARTA SCHWARZOVÁ   PHA 16.2.47

When one does not have what one loves, one loves what one has.

:: MARTA SCHWARZOVÁ   PRG 02.16.47

Mariánka saw Marta Schwarzová, a former Terezín inmate, again in Prague after the war. Schwarzová enjoyed the luxury of a bathtub in her apartment, and Mariánka occasionally took a bath there.

Quand on n'a pas ce que l'on aime,
on aime ce que l'on a.

[signature]

Pka, 16.2.47.

100

Zur Erinnerung an Ihre erste „Bekannte" in schlechter Zeit, Dresdner Kaserne Z. 188.

Das allerbeste für die Zukunft.

:: IHRE
MARIANNE HOLZER
TH. 16. VI. 1945

In memory of your first "acquaintance" during bad times, Dresden Barracks, Rm. 188.

Wishing you the very best for the future.

:: YOURS
MARIANNA HOLZER
TH. 06.16. 1945

Marianne Holzer was born 22 December 1900 and deported from Prague to Terezín on 14 December 1941. She survived three and a half years of incarceration and was liberated in the transit camp. Mariánka remembers her as "one of the few nice women with whom we shared the FLOOR of room 188—like sardines—" in Dresden barracks, their first lodging. Mariánka and Hilda later moved to Hamburg barracks and, finally, to Jägergasse 9.

Zur Erinnerung
an Ihre erste „Bekannte"
in schlechter Zeit, Dresdner
Kaserne Z.188. –
Das Allerbeste für die
Zukunft Ihre

Marianne Hobre

Pk. 16. VI. 1945

IOI

Život je malá bílá loď, která se houpá,
Ve víru osudu se zmítá sem a tam . . .
Buď naší malou lodí někde zakotvíme
Anebo s námi někde ztroskotá.

Přeji Vám, Mariánko, abyste
někde pevně a štástně zakotvila.
Ve vzpomínce na dlouhá
společná léta v těžké době.

:: EDITA PICKOVÁ   V PRAZE, I8. XI.I945

Life is a small, white ship that keeps on rocking
In the whirlpool of fate it spins to and fro . . .
Either we drop somewhere the ship's anchor
Or we may end up shipwrecked with it.

I wish you, Mariánka, a secure and happy landing.
In memory of the long years we spent together during
difficult times.

:: EDITA PICKOVÁ   IN PRAGUE, II.I8. I945

Edita Picková and Mariánka were friends in Terezín, and they met again in Prague after the war,
but only once. Both Edita and her mother Paula (entry 102) survived.

Život je malá, bílá loď, která se
houpá,
Ve víru osudu se zmítá sem a tam......
Buď s naší malou lodí někde
zakotvíme
Anebo s námi někde ztroskotá.

Přeji Vám, Mariánko, abyste
někde pevně a šťastně zakotvila.

Ve vzpomínce na dlouhá
společná léta v těžké době
Edita Pišková

v Praze, 18. XI. 1945.

102

Es ist kein Glück so rein, so tief,
Daß nicht eine Träne mit unterlief.
Es ist so groß, so lange kein Weh,
Daß nicht eine Hoffnung darüber geh'.

Der lieben, tapfern, kleinen Marianne zur Erinnerung
an eine von den wenigen übriggebliebenen Baben aus
Theresienstadt. :: PAULA PICK   PRAG, D. 18. NOVEMBER 1945

There is no happiness so pure, so deep
That not one tear would not appear.
No pain is as great and extended
That there would not be a chance for hope as well.

To dear, brave, little Marianne so that she would remember
one of the few of old women still left in Theresienstadt.
:: PAULA PICK   PRAGUE, 18 NOVEMBER 1945

Paula Pick, born 21 April 1880, and her daughter Edita (entry 101), born 18 March 1905, were deported from Prague to Terezín on 12 May 1942. They were among the few mother-daughter pairs to survive in the transit camp until liberation. Edita and Mariánka had been friends in Terezín, and mother and daughter visited her in Prague once; they signed her album on that occasion.

Es ist kein Glück so rein, so tief,
Das nicht eine Träne mit unterlief.
Es ist so groß, so bange kein Weh,
Das nicht eine Hoffnung darüber geh'.

Der lieben, tapfern, kleinen Marianne
zur Erinnerung an eine von den wenigen
übriggebliebenen Baben aus Theresienstadt.

Paula Pick.

Prag, d. 18. November 1945.

103

Ich habe imer Maenni beneidet, daß ein so schönes, herziges
Mädel ihn libet. Ich werde imer wieder es wiederholen: Dů bist
ein lieber Kerl, ein nettes Mädel, ein Mensch, der wert ist,
geliebt zu werden.

:: IN ALTER FREUNDSCHAFT, DR. ERNST FELDSBERG   TEREZÍN, 25.V.45

I always felt envious of Maenni that such a beautiful, lovely girl
loved him. Time and again I shall repeat: You are a dear person,
a very nice girl, a being who deserves to be loved.

:: IN OLD FRIENDSHIP, DR. ERNST FELDSBERG   TEREZÍN, 05.25.45

*Ernst Feldsberg survived the Holocaust and returned to Austria after the war. He became the
executive director of the Jewish community of Vienna. In his entry, Feldsberg refers to a young
Danish man, Maenni Ruben (see entry 90).*

Ich habe immer Maenni
beneidet, dass ein so
schönes, herziges Mädel ihn
liebt.

Ich werde immer wieder
es wiederholen:
Du bist ein lieber Kerl,
ein nettes Mädel,
ein Mensch, der wert ist,
    geliebt zu werden.

In alter Freundschaft
Dr Ernst Feldsberg

Terezin – 25. V. 45

104

Vzpomínka je jediný ráj, z něhož nemůžeme byti vyhnáni.

:: V UPOMÍNKU VEPSALA TVÁ TĚ MILUJÍCÍ ANDULA

INTELIGENT

DNE 4./II.1946

Memory is the only paradise from which we cannot be expelled.

:: IN MEMORY INSCRIBED BY YOUR LOVING ANDULA

INTELLIGENT

02.04.1946

A former Terezín inmate, Andula was Mariánka's co-worker at the Jewish Community Center in Prague after the war.

Vzpomínka je jediný ráj,
z něhož nemůžeme býti
vyhnáni.

Vzpomínku
vepsala tvá tě milující

Andula
inteligent

dne 4/II. 1946.

105

Liebes Mariandl, dass ich Dich kennen lernte, hat mich sehr sehr
gefreut und ich wünsche Dir alles Gute für Deine Zukunft!

:: MARIANNE FRÖHLICH   THERESIENSTADT, 10. JUNI 1945

Dear Mariandl, I am very very glad that I got to know you and I
wish you all the best for your future!

:: MARIANNE FRÖHLICH   THERESIENSTADT, 10 JUNE 1945

This is a second entry by Marianne Fröhlich. See entry 18.

Liebes Mariandl, dass ich Dir kennen lernte, hat mich sehr sehr gefreut und ich wünsche Dir alles Gute für Deine Zukunft!

Marianne Froehlich

Theresienstadt, 10. Juni 1945

106

Marianko—žili jsme v Terezíně přece nějakým životem,
nezapomeň na Verdiovo „Requiem" a na „basistu."

:: OTA WOLFE V PRAZE 12/XI. 1945

Mariánka—we lived nevertheless some kind of life in Terezín.
Do not forget Verdi's "Requiem" and the "basso."

:: OTA WOLFE IN PRAGUE, 11.12.1945

Ota (Otto) Wolfe headed the mica barracks by day and sang in Schächter's chorus after hours. Deported to Auschwitz, Wolfe survived. He and Mariánka saw each other again in Prague and kept in contact through the 1990s. Wolfe and Mariánka met in 1990 at Carnegie Hall upon the occasion of a memorial performance of Verdi's Requiem. *Conducted by Robert DeCormier and introduced by Rabbi Alexander Schindler (then president of the Union of American Hebrew Congregations), the concert was dedicated to the singers, instrumentalists, and conductor who had performed* The Requiem *in Terezín in 1944.*

Marianko – žili jsme v
Terezíně péče nějakým životem,
vzpomeň na Verdiovo „Requiem"
a na „bassistu"

V Praze dne 12/XI.1945.

107

V Terezíně sice ještě, ale již na svobodě, přeji Vám, milá
Mariánko, abyste nové naší svobody užila v dalším Vašem životě
ve štěstí a zdraví, a co možno nejdéle ve společnosti Vaší mně
tak milé matinky. :: MÁŇA KLEINOVÁ   7.V.1945

Although still in Terezín but already free, I wish, dear Mariánka, that
you enjoy our new freedom in your future life in happiness and in
health, and hopefully as long as possible in the company of your dear
mother of whom I am so fond. :: MÁŇA KLEINOVÁ   05.07.1945

Máňa Kleinová, a typist, had studied art with Hilda Zadikow, and the two women were friends.

7. V. 1945.

V Terezíně sice ještě, ale již
na svobodě, přeji Vám, milá Mariánko,
abyste nové naší svobody užila v
dalším Vašem životě ve štěstí a
zdraví, a co možno nejdéle ve společnosti Vaší mně tak milé matinky.

Máňa Kleinová

108

Sousedce Mariánce v upomínku,

:: LOTKA BUREŠOVÁ   13.11.1944

To my neighbor Mariánka as a memento,

:: LOTKA BUREŠOVÁ   11.13.1944

Lotka (Charlotta) Burešová (b. 4 November 1904) was deported to Terezín on 20 July 1942. She worked with Hilda Zadikow in the Lautsch company workshops, and she and the Zadikows were quartered in the same building at Jägergasse 9 (their third and last address in Terezín). A professional artist in Prague before the war, she brought art supplies with her when she was deported to Terezín. Her husband, a gentile, maintained contact with her through the postal system, periodically sending her food packages with hidden art supplies. Among the pictures Burešová drew clandestinely in Terezín is a portrait of the movie actor and director Kurt Gerron. It is probably the last image of a man much photographed before the war. Gerron was deported to Auschwitz in October 1944, where he was killed. Burešová survived and was liberated in Terezín.

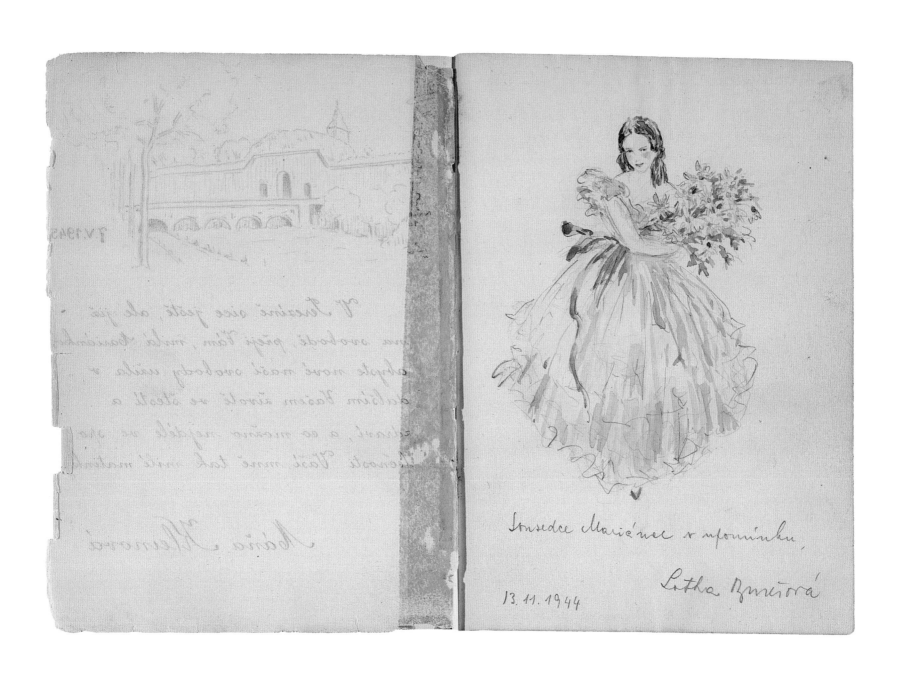

Sousedce Mariénce v upomínku,

Litka Bznerová

13. 11. 1944

109

{ VERSO }

Vzpomínka na slavné zkoušky u Karla.

:: EVA V TEREZÍNĚ 23/VI 1945

In memory of the glorious rehearsals at Karel's.

:: EVA IN TEREZÍN, 06.23.1945

{ RECTO }

Heim kommt man nie, aber wo befreundete Wege zusammen laufen, da sieht die ganze Welt für eine Stunde wie Heimat aus.

Zur Erinnerung an die in Theresienstadt 1945 begonnene Freundschaft.

:: PH.MGR. RUDI PICK

HANNE MARIE PICK

One never reaches Home, but where friendly paths meet, the whole world looks like Home for an hour.

In memory of our friendship that started in 1945 in Terezín.

:: PHARMACIST RUDI PICK

HANNE MARIE PICK

Eva was a member of Schächter's chorus. She and Mariánka rehearsed under Karel Berman's direction.

Rudi Pick worked in his profession as a pharmacist in Terezín. He was also gifted at repairing musical instruments. Signed by him and his wife Hanne Marie, the text is a quote from Hermann Hesse.

† Terezíně 23/VI 1945

Vzpomínka na tamní
akustiky u Karla
Čmo.

Heim kommt man nie,
Aber wo befreundete Wege zu-
sammenlaufen, da sieht
die ganze Welt für eine
Stunde wie Heimat aus.

Zur Erinnerung an
die in Theresienstadt
1945 begonnene Freund-
schaft.

Ph.Dr. Rudi Pick
Hanne Marie Pick

IIO

Rád si budu vždy vzpomínat na Marjánku.

:: LEO KOLLINSKÝ   24/6 1945

I shall always be glad to remember Mariánka.

:: LEO KOLLINSKÝ   06.24.1945

Leo Kollinský, born 11 February 1893, was deported to Terezín from Prague on 5 July 1943. Kollinský was in charge of the agricultural department in the transit camp. He was affectionately called strejda *(uncle) by Mariánka and others. He survived and was liberated in Terezín.*

Rád si budu
vždy vzpomínat
na Marjánku.

Leo Kollinský

24/6 1945.

III

Tempora mutantur, mutamur et nos in illis.

:: RICHARD LUDWIG MARENS   TEREZÍN 24.VI.1945

Times change, we change in them.

:: RICHARD LUDWIG MARENS   TEREZÍN, 06.24.1945

Richard Ludwig Marens was a beekeeper in Terezín. He and his wife survived. Mariánka respected him greatly, and the two liked each other very much.

Tempora mutantur,
mutamur et nos
in illis.

Richard Ludwig Marcay

Torino 24. II 1845

112

Wer durch die
Theresienstädter „Schleussen
u. Auslese" ging ohne grossen
Schaden zu nehmen, wurde
vom lieben Gott auserwählt.

:: FILI HERRLICH
THERESIENSTADT, 21.5.45

Whoever passed through the
Theresienstadt "sluices and
selections" without major
harm must have been selected
by dear God himself.

:: FILI HERRLICH
THERESIENSTADT, 05.21.45

Fili Herrlich and Mariánka worked together in the fields in the spring of 1945. Much earlier, they were quartered together in the Dresden barracks, where they slept on the bare floor. (See entry 100.) In her entry, Fili Herrlich refers to the arrival in Terezín at the "sluice" and the numerous "selections" for deportation to the east.

Wer durch die Theresienstädter
„Schleussen u. Auslese" ging
ohne grossen Schaden zu
nehmen,
wurde vom lieben Gott
auserwählt.

Fili Herrlich.

Theresienstadt, 21.5.45.

113

Na památku na zlaté časy „Landwirtschaftské".

:: TVÁ EMKA V TEREZÍNĚ 30/5. 45

In memory of the golden times in "Landwirtschaft" [agricultural
work detail]. :: YOUR EMKA IN TEREZÍN, 05.30.45

*Emka and Mariánka worked in the same agricultural work detail in April 1945, just before
liberation.*

Na památku
na zlaté časy
„Landwirtschaftka"

Tvá Ema

v Terezíně 30/5.45.

114

Moje Mariánko, jen jedno přání mám, za všechno dobré, ať
Tě provází Pán Bůh sám.

:: MAMA ČÁNSKÁ PRAHA 11/8.1946

My Mariánka, I have only one wish, for all our good deeds
may the Lord Himself be by your side.

:: MOM ČÁNSKÁ PRAGUE, 08.11.1946

Mariánka met Čánská in Prague after the war. She remembers her as a person who took care of anyone in need.

Praha 11/8. 1946.

Moji Mariánko,

jen jedno přání máme,
za všechno dobré, ať Ti
prováší Pán Bůh pán.

máma Čánska!

115

Doufám, že Terezín nezapomenem. Pak se nám nenavrátí.

:: TVŮJ W. BORGES   9.7.46

I hope that we never forget Terezín. Then it cannot return to us.

:: YOUR W. BORGES   07.09.46

An engineer by profession, W. (Wolfi, or Wolfgang, or Bedřich) Borges (b. 28 August 1909) was a talented bass singer. He was deported from Prague to Terezín on 4 December 1941, probably with one of the construction crews (Aufbaukommandos) to build the camp. A worker by day, he participated in the cultural life of Terezín by night. Borges played Kecal in Schächter's production of The Bartered Bride *until the professional singer Karel Berman took over the part. Terezín hosted enough performances to use all available talent: he sang opposite Marion Podolier in* La serva padrona, *and Mariánka remembers him as Figaro in* The Marriage of Figaro. *Borges was deported to Auschwitz on 28 September 1944 and was liberated in the subcamp in Blechhammer. The music in his entry is from* The Bartered Bride. *Wolfi Borges and Mariánka remained friendly in Prague after the war, and this entry dates from that time.*

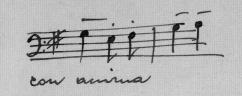

con anima

Doufám, že Terezín nezapomenem. Pak se nám nenavrátí.

Tvůj

W. Borges

9. 7. 46

116

Každý král má svou královnu,
Každý Bůh má své nebe . . .
a já mám Tebe!!

:: RODEK   PRAHA   15/XII 1946

Every king has his queen,
Every god has his heaven . . .
and I have you!!

:: RODEK   PRAGUE   12. 15. 1946

Originally from Prague, Rodek served with the British army and returned to his native city after the war.

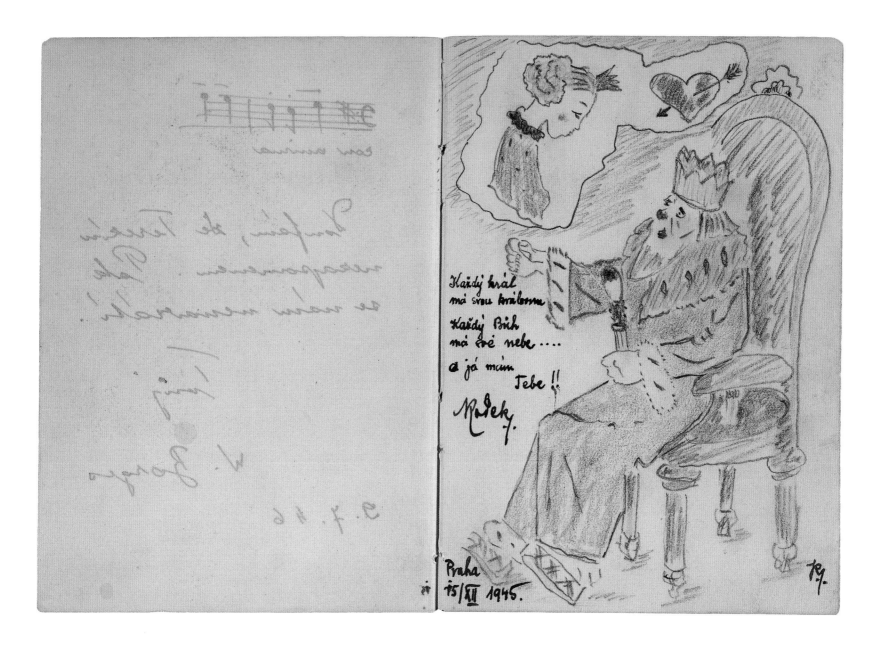

Každý král
má svou králonu
Každý Bůh
má své nebe....
a já mám
Tebe !!
Radek.

Praha
15/XII 1945.

117

Mariánko, přála bych si jen, abychom na sebe nikdy nezapomněly!

A což datum 3. x.44?

Mariánka, I would only wish that we never forget one another!

And how about the date 10.03.44?

The four sets of initials on the music staff refer to Mariánka Zadikow and her friends Nina Schwarz (also called Schwarzová, see entry 34 recto), Eva Wesecky, and Hanka Steindler, all of whom sang in Schächter's chorus. Eva Wesecky got a deportation notice while she was writing in the Poesiealbum. *Transport "En" to Auschwitz did indeed leave the following day (4 October 1944), but Wesecky was not on it. She, like the other three young women, remained in Terezín until liberation. Mariánka has maintained contact with all of them.*

Mariánko, přála bych si jen,
abychom na sebe nikdy nezapomněly!

A což datum 3.X.44?

118

Schubert Fantasie f-moll

Zur Erinnerung an die holländische Hälfte des
Tereziner Klavier-duos und hoffentlich bald „Auf
Wiederhören" in Holland!

:: BÉ PIMENTEL   TEREZÍN, 6/6 '45

Schubert, Fantasie in F Minor

To remember the Dutch half of the Terezín
piano-duos and hopefully we may "hear each
other soon" in Holland!

:: BÉ PIMENTAL   TEREZÍN, 06.06.45

Was man scheint, hat jederman zum Richter,
Was man ist, hat keinen.

:: ERNST BÖHM   THERESIENSTADT, AM 21. JUNI 1945

What one seems to be is being judged by many,
what one really is has no judge.

:: ERNST BÖHM   THERESIENSTADT, 21 JUNE 1945

Deported to Terezín from the Netherlands, Bé (Beatrice) Pimentel was an excellent pianist who performed solo and in four-hand piano duets with others, particularly Edith Steiner-Kraus.

Ernst Böhm worked in the Galanteriewarenerzeugung *(notions workshop) with Mariánka.*

[Left page]

Schubert
Fantasie f-moll

[musical notation]

Zur Erinne-
rung an die
holländische Hälfte
des Terezíner Kla-
vier-duos und hof-
fentlich bald
"auf Wiederhören"
in Holland!

[signature]

Terezín, 6/6 '45.

[Right page]

Was man scheint, hat jederman zum Richter,
Das man ist, hat keinen.

Ernst Böhm.

Theresienstadt, am 21. Juni 1945

119

Milé spolupracovnici na trvalou vzpomínku.

:: DR. STEIN V PRAZE   5. DUBNA 46

To a dear co-worker as a lasting memento.

:: DR. STEIN IN PRAGUE   5 APRIL 46

Dr. Stein was the chairman of the Jewish Community Center in Prague.

v Praze.

Miłe sp[o]tkanie ornici
na trwałą pamiątkę
5. dubna 46.

120

Daří-li se ti v životě dobře, můžeš zapomenout; Potřebuješ-li
ale někdy v životě někoho, nezapomeň na upřímného člověka a
přítele. :: DAVID GRÜNZWEIG PRAHA 28.V.1946.

If life treats you well, you may as well forget; but should you ever
need someone, do not forget a sincere friend and a good friend.

:: DAVID GRÜNZWEIG PRAGUE, 05.28.1946

*David Grünzweig (b. 2 June 1879) was deported with the last transport from Prague to Terezín
on 16 March 1945 and returned to the city after liberation. He was very fond of Mariánka.*

Daří-li se ti v životě
dobře, můžeš zapomenouti;.
Potřebuješ-li ale někdy v životě
někoho, nezapomeň na
upřímného člověka a
přítele.
David Grünweig

Praha 28. V. 1946.

121

Meiner Konkurentin in Freizeitbesuchen zur Erinnerung von

:: D. LOKESCH TH., 11.IV.45

To my dear rival at free-time visits as a memento from

:: D. LOKESCH TH. 04.11.45

Dr. Lokesch was a physician, a music lover, and a good friend to Mariánka in Terezín.

Meiner Konkurrentin
in Freizeit besuchen zur
Erinnerung an
[Signatur]
B., 11. IV. 45.

122

Met mijn bijzondere hoogachting voor de Dames Zadikow.

:: H. COHEN   HOLLAND   20 MEI 1945

With my utmost respect for the Zadikow ladies.

:: H. COHEN   HOLLAND   20 MAY 1945

Hartog Cohen lived in the same building as Mariánka and her mother. All the inhabitants of Jägergasse 9 were painters except Mariánka. Cohen "saved me from a Russian soldier who was just about to rape me," Mariánka recalled. "He was already on top of me. Put down his rifle, held the pistol, and he weighed maybe three hundred pounds with all his army kit. But he forgot to put his hand over my mouth so I screamed. [Hartog Cohen] lived in the same house, an old, old man with the hands of a butcher . . . And he grabbed him and threw him out." Mariánka assumes the soldier was too surprised to shoot Cohen.

Met mijn byzondere hoogachting

Voor de Dames ZADIKOW

H. Cohen

Holland

20 Mei 1945

123

Meine kleine liebe schöne Mathilda Zadikow
mit viele schöne Grüsse

:: DAAN PIMENTEL   THERESIENSTADT 1/6 45

My little dear beautiful Mathilda Zadikow
With many lovely greetings

:: DAAN PIMENTEL   THERESIENSTADT 06.01.45

Daan Pimentel, father of Bé Pimentel (entry 118 verso), was an artist who lived in the same building at Jägergasse 9 as Hartog Cohen (entry 122) and Hilda and Mariánka. He was nearly blind by the time he wrote this entry.

Theresienstadt 1

meine Kleine 6...

liebe schöne

Mathilda Zadikow

mit viele Schöne

Grüsse

Daan Pimente